Seeking Saúl

An American Mother's Journey to Colombia

Rebecca Thatcher Murcia

By

REBECCA THATCHER MURCIA

About the Author

Rebecca Thatcher Murcia graduated from the University of Massachusetts and worked at newspapers in Northampton, Mass., Brownsville, Texas, and Austin, Texas, before moving to Pennsylvania in 2001. Her husband, Saúl Murcia, grew up on a farm in Colombia and went to Goshen College in Indiana. The two met in Brownsville in 1989. Thatcher Murcia is also the author of *Américo Paredes, Carl Sandburg, We Visit Colombia, The Civil Rights Movement,* and 14 other books for children and young adults, all published by Mitchell Lane.

For Gabriel and Mario:
You have been fantastic examples during the last few years.
You have lived in the moment and you
have shown a lot of courage.
Thank you.

Table of Contents

Prologue

The waiting area of the Lancaster County Department of Transportation was not a happy place to be on a lovely June afternoon. The floor was covered with ugly government-issue tile. The walls were the yellow of dry heaves. There were no plants or décor to even pretend that this was anywhere to bring my mother and my two boys, who sat quietly in plastic molded chairs.

"I can take them to the dollar store if you'd like," offered my mother.

"Thanks," I nodded, hardly hearing her. I was there, but not really. We all remained in our chairs.

"*Rebecca Thatcher*," called the clerk at last.

At the counter, I explained that my license had expired. "And in addition to renewing it," I said, "I would like to change my last name to Murcia."

The clerk eyed me with suspicion. "What makes you think you can do that?" he asked.

I pulled out the battered marriage license that had been signed and witnessed 16 years earlier, then mailed to "Mr. and Mrs. Saúl Murcia" by a Cameron County, Texas, functionary. When Saul and I married in 1989 I was a 27-year-old hard-charging investigative reporter with no plans of changing the name I was trying to make for myself. Now, as I handed over the document that I had stuffed into a file so many years ago in Brownsville, Texas, I tried not to think of my second date with Saúl, how he had cooked me a delicious dinner and then we sat on my couch for hours, telling each other about our lives. When he suddenly drew me to him and kissed me with passion, I felt tremors all through my body. We went our separate ways that night but we couldn't stop thinking about each other.

I worked at the *Brownsville Herald,* covering a Central American refugee crisis that was creating national headlines. Saúl, a native of Colombia, was a volunteer at the Mennonite church, meeting with refugee after refugee, helping them fill out forms, and providing them with simple meals. Despite the chaos of the times, we spent all our free time together. He drew me into his circle of volunteers who worked at the public health clinics and low-income legal offices of the Rio Grande Valley. And Saúl spent time with my reporter friends as we tried to keep abreast of the volatile crisis. Refugees flooded into South Texas after President Ronald Reagan announced that he considered all Nicaraguans as legitimate exiles of a totalitarian Sandinista revolution. They were often caught by the Border Patrol and instructed to wait in the local area while their cases were decided.

After just a few months, Saúl and I decided to marry.

We wrote our wedding vows together, in English and Spanish, and promised to be lovers to each other forever and ever.

Standing before the clerk, I tried not to think of my memories of Saúl holding my hand and teaching my clumsy North American feet to move to sensuous rhythms of Colombian *salsa.* I steered my mind away from the hundreds of delicious dishes Saúl had cooked for me, effortlessly whipping together whatever was in the fridge into delicious mouthfuls, heavy with the rich flavors of onions, garlic and cilantro.

I focused on the clerk's mannerisms as he studied the ornate writing on the Texas marriage certificate. He touched the raised golden seal, practically sniffing for clues as to the document's authenticity. At last, he relented. "So how exactly do you want your name to read now?"

I tensed, drew a breath. I did not want to burst into tears at that dingy office or, for that matter, yet another time on that lovely June day. I steadied myself to answer his question.

"Rebecca Thatcher Murcia," I said, using all my strength not to falter.

The clerk had no more questions. For that, I was grateful. Saúl Murcia, my dear husband, had been dead for eight days.

One

Our Life in Six Suitcases

All of Colombia's history has been a matter of surviving difficult times. Our grandparents and our parents suffered from the violence at the end of the 1940s and they had to flee their farms and take up new lives in the cities. In other words, 50 years ago, they suffered from the same violence that today has driven more than 3 million Colombians from their homes.
From Saúl Murcia's 2004 letter

There we were, fresh off of the six-hour, non-stop flight from New York: a tall, blond American soccer mom in her best new black khakis and polo shirt, her two boys, a small brown-and-white dog in a portable kennel, and everything we would need or that we could stuff into six bulging suitcases—for a year in South America.

The dog began to whimper.

"Is anybody going to pick us up?" asked Mario.

"Of course," I said with false cheer. "They probably just got delayed."

Now was not the time to admit that I couldn't remember whether in the whirlwind of preparing for this adventure I had remembered to call my sister-in-law and let her know what time we were arriving.

The crowds that had been on the sidewalk in front of the international airport in Bogotá were thinning out. The sky was cloudy and a slight breeze kept the air moving; it was a typically cool day in the Colombian capital, which occupies a high plane between two ridges of the forbidding Andes Mountains.

Mario, 10, had just finished fourth grade, and Gabriel, 12, had graduated from sixth grade back in Pennsylvania. I would have just enough time to scout out new schools and enroll them for the 2007 Colombian fall semester. All we needed was someone to pick us up.

The porter looked at me curiously. His cart was overflowing with our six suspiciously stuffed suitcases. I had crammed in as much clothing, electronics and sports equipment as possible; you could practically trace the outline of the soccer balls bulging at the sides of one of the suitcases. One suitcase was solely reserved for books, many of them hardcover; I could hardly meet the porter's eyes out of guilt.

The minutes dragged by and the excitement of getting up at 2:30 a.m. to catch the flight was waning. The boys kept sighing exaggeratedly to show their impatience, and I could hear the agitated toenail sounds of Crystal trying to get comfortable in her little kennel. I too was exhausted, confused, even a little scared. But I remained calm, as was my habit since becoming the only parent of these two boys.

I tried to remember, though ... did I actually tell anyone what flight we were on? Between renting out our house in Akron, hauling the possessions that did not fit into six suitcases to a locked storage room, and handing over the reins of the boys' soccer team I had been coaching to three volunteer dads, perhaps I had missed this one item?

"What do we do if nobody shows up?" asked Gabriel.

What indeed? We had just flown 2,473 miles with everything we held dear. Everything we held dear that was left, anyway.

Saúl Murcia, a native of this land, my husband of 16 years and the father of my two sons, fought a horrible case of bone cancer for two years before dying in June of 2005. Gabriel was nine; Mario was eight and we were all heartbroken.

We buried Saúl on a lovely hill overlooking the tidy farms of Lancaster County. We placed flowers and origami peace cranes on the coffin as family and neighborhood friends stood with us. We sang an old hymn from Saúl's childhood in Colombia: *"I heard a voice from heaven and it said, 'My child, don't take too long to arrive.'"*

Then I rose to my feet. I had not prepared a speech, but I needed to cut through the usual euphemisms that are used for comfort in a time like this.

"We are heartbroken over Saúl's death," I began. "He did not 'pass away' and he did not 'negotiate the river Jordan.' He became very ill from a disease he fought with every ounce of his being. It killed him anyway, and for that we are devastated, hurt, bereft."

The reception was at Saúl's former office, where they had laid out a simple spread of fruit, cookies and coffee. Barry Kreider, the pastor of our church, Pilgrim's Mennonite, folded his lanky frame into the chair beside us. He was helping organize a memorial service to take place two days later.

"What do you think is the best way to honor Saúl?" he asked.

Gabriel did not hesitate.

"A big soccer game," he announced.

"Sweetie, I don't know if you can have soccer at a funeral," I said.

"But he would like it!" Gabriel insisted.

Barry didn't seem perturbed, although this must have been a first for him, or for anyone. And so, after a beautiful service, in which people sang, played instruments, spoke of their love for Saúl and told funny stories about his life, some 40 of us walked from the church down the hill to a field and played soccer. So many of us played that there were two balls on the field at once. When a farmer's wife—a conservative young Mennonite wearing the proper white head covering and a long cotton print dress—dribbled both balls down the field, she was admired as if she were Pelé in a dress.

Saúl had studied as a child at a Mennonite boarding school in Colombia and later graduated from Goshen College, a Mennonite institution in Indiana. He worked for Mennonite service organizations all his life. Before his death, he was co-director for Latin America for the Mennonite Central Committee, an agency that promoted peace and development throughout the world.

The Mennonite church began with Menno Simons, an early 16th-century priest who became disillusioned with Catholicism and joined the Anabaptists, who were, in defiance of the authorities, baptizing adults who had decided to follow Jesus. Since then, Mennonites have divided into groups ranging from the horse-and-buggy conservative Mennonites, who are nearly as anti-technology as the Amish, to the more liberal modern wing that sponsors missionaries and service projects globally. We were modern Mennonites. I joined the church when I married Saúl, who still remembered the name of the Mennonite missionary from Indiana who taught him how to read.

Saúl's Colombian parents were inconsolable over his death but they did not come to the burial or the memorial service. His two sisters and one brother who lived in Colombia were likewise not able to make the trip.

A few weeks after the funeral, even though I was still in a fog of grief, the boys and I went to Colombia to spend a few weeks visiting Saúl's parents at the farm where my husband grew up, and also went to see Saúl's brother, Edilberto, a city engineer in Bogotá, his sister Gloria, a teacher in La Mesa near the farm, and another sister Flor, a Christian radio psychologist.

Gabriel has my gummy smile and Mario has my green eyes, but they also strongly resemble Saúl, and that must have been a comforting sight for the family.

"I'm so glad we came here, even if it seems so soon to travel," I told Flor one afternoon over coffee in her elegant Bogotá apartment, while Gabriel and Mario played computer games in the guest room.

"I wonder if you'd consider a longer visit," said Flor. "Maybe bring the boys to live here for a year, so they could spend more time with us."

I nodded, but it was way too much to think about right then.

A few days after that, we went to see Saúl's sister, Gloria, at her house in La Mesa, population 30,000. Gloria lives on the south side in Comfenalco, a compact neighborhood of townhouses, with two little playgrounds and a cement soccer field. The complex was built to house the hard-working but poorly-paid public school teachers.

We were kicking a ball around the soccer court in front of Gloria's house when some kids asked us to join in a game. We played and played that afternoon. Whenever I got the ball, some kid would yell, "Be careful! She can play!" My Spanish was good enough to catch the warning, which I took as a compliment.

An hour after the game started, there was a crowd of children watching from the sidelines, waiting their turn. The older kids decided to form a third team and have three teams take turns playing each other. They chose the first captain and the second captain, and then they needed a third captain.

"Gabriel, you be a captain," said one of the older kids.

Gabriel smiled shyly. "*Está bien,*" he said.

The boys seemed fine on their own, so I went inside to help Gloria with dinner. And I didn't want an opportunity to relive those bad memories of being picked last for baseball games when I was 11.

That night at the dinner table, the boys talked excitedly about playing with the neighborhood children.

"They were so nice to include us right from the beginning," I told Gloria.

"Oh, this is a great place," said Gloria. "A lot of good families, and most of the parents are teachers."

Soon it was time to return to Akron and look for a new normal as a family of three. I read a book called *Guiding Your Child Through Grief* and tried to heed its advice to be supportive and available to my children. I watched them for signs of depression, but they were more like good examples to me of living in the moment, treasuring Saúl's memory and yet accepting his death.

As I struggled through that first year as a widow, Flor's idea kept kicking around in my mind. Saúl had alluded to fascinating stories of growing up on the farm outside La Mesa, about getting up at 2 a.m. to mill sugar cane and breaking teeth in a soccer game in school.

When Ana María, the lovely daughter of one of Saúl's favorite cousins, came to visit, we sat together reading pages and pages of letters that Saúl had written to his family when he was first diagnosed with cancer. He left the letters on the hard drive of the computer we shared, but never talked about them with me. Although I could understand the general gist of them, Saúl used a lot of Colombian colloquialisms. It was a significant help having the literate Ana María on hand to help translate. I remember being annoyed with Saúl for taking hours and hours away from the family to work on these letters during his recovery from surgery. But now I treasured the vivid writing and the recollection of a Colombian childhood that I knew little about.

One of the letters contained a long story about a senior class train trip to the Colombian coast—the birthplace of *vallenato*, a fast-paced, accordion-based music that former Colombian soap opera actor Carlos Vives has made internationally famous. Saúl's boyhood friend Nelson, who lived on the neighboring farm, secretly introduced him to *vallenato*. Thereafter, the two boys would sneak away each weekend to listen to their favorite *vallenato* show on the radio, out of earshot of their very conservative, evangelical parents.

"For Nelson and me, listening to *vallenatos* was like a clandestine vice," Saúl wrote after his first cancer surgery. "We lived it quietly, since among so many converted Christians there were plenty who were very concerned about the temptations of the flesh, and our daring to do this could well have landed us in front of the congregation to confess a sin. Without realizing it, Nelson gave me the way to survive my exile from Colombia, now for half a lifetime with hints of impending doom. I've always remembered my special time of adoring *vallenato* with Nelson, in times when I'm missing Colombia. It was then, when the *vallenatos* slaked a thirst for home and an internal recrimination for having left."

An internal recrimination for having left. I read those words over and over again. Saúl had never admitted to me that he regretted leaving Colombia. *If Saúl regretted leaving, he would be happy about us going back, right?* I thought to myself. I became more inspired to take my children to live in their father's country.

There was also the notebook. The day Saúl's cancer doctor told us his cancer was incurable, I screwed up the courage to ask him to think about what he wanted for his children and write it down. We were driving home from the dreadful meeting with his cancer doctor at Johns Hopkins Hospital in Maryland. "Sweetie, I know you cannot bear to talk about us going on without you, but please think about it and write down what you want for your sons."

"Okay," he said. "I do want to do something like that." I looked at his stoic profile as he guided the car up Interstate 83. I wished he would tell me about the pain he was feeling, but I knew him too well to expect that. I never brought it up again. Saúl simply could not bear to talk about his death.

But I did find a notebook where Saúl had scribbled some thoughts about Gabriel and Mario. He included something he obviously wanted to say to his older son about soccer. "Soccer is not everything in life [but] the methods here in Pennsylvania/USA are the worst… Everything is very structured. You should play for fun without so much structure."

"Also you should think of other social things: study, church, and not spend time traveling all over to games."

Reading those few scribbled lines did not give me confidence that Saúl would have been thrilled about us going to his country. But I did think that at least Saúl was underscoring the importance of learning to play soccer the way he did, without registrations or teams or leagues or lots of travel, but just by playing for fun with friends.

A few weeks later, Gabriel was having his customary glass of milk with Oreos at the dining room table after school. I gingerly told him I was think-ing about moving to Colombia for a year—maybe at some point in the fu-ture. I had decided a year made more sense than say, a summer. If we went for a year we could lease our house and get somebody to pay the mortgage rather than pay somebody to take care of it. But more importantly, I was sure that Gabriel and Mario would really master Spanish if we stayed in Colombia for a year.

"Let's do it now, Mom," he said, washing down his Oreos with some milk. "I want to be back here for eighth grade, when soccer starts to get serious."

I exhaled with relief. I was surprised and glad that Gabriel was open to doing something so outrageous, even though he spoke better Spanish than Mario. When the boys were young, Saúl and I tried to speak to them in Spanish all the time, figuring that they'd get all the English they needed in pre-school. It worked perfectly for Gabriel, who spoke mostly Spanish until he went to pre-school at three. But Mario started preschool at two and, although he un-derstood Spanish fairly well, he still struggled to speak it.

"Just one thing," added Gabriel, wiping his mouth with the back of his sleeve like I'd told him not to and leaving a black trail of Oreo crumbs on it. "We're bringing Crystal. I won't go without her."

Saúl's partner at the Mennonite Central Committee, Daryl, had dropped off a terrier-type dog at our house when Saúl was ill. Daryl's children were away at college and, for some reason, Daryl thought I needed a dog to take care of as well as two boys and a husband who had been rendered an invalid by ter-minal cancer. Gabriel and Mario immediately fell in love with Crystal. Despite my reluctance, we let her stay. I had seen dogs on the airplane the last time we had gone to Colombia, so I thought I could grant Gabriel this one wish.

Breaking the news to Mario later that evening wasn't as easy. "Mario, I've decided we're going to Colombia for a year," I said.

Mario responded as quickly as Gabriel had, only differently. He hurled himself onto his bed and sobbed with his face in both hands.

"What is it, sweetie?" I asked, kneeling at his bedside. "Is it about the Spanish?" "Yes," he said, his voice muffled through his hands and his tears. "Plus my friends!" Mario's three closest buddies would be at Akron Elementary School.

I felt terrible, but I also knew that the reason Mario had such close friends in Akron was because he was so good at connecting with people. He would undoubtedly make new friends in Colombia.

I spent the whole next year getting ready. The biggest obstacle was the Colombian government. Doris, a cousin of Saúl's who thought the trip was a great idea, went to the Colombian consulate in New York to find out about visa requirements.

"Impossible," pronounced a truculent official. "She can only go to Colombia for a year if she is studying full-time at a Colombian university."

I moped around the house for a few days. Then I decided I would not take no for an answer and began scouring the Colombian government's website for other categories for extended visas. It did not look good. There were visas for every possible category except mine: Widows of Colombians Who Want Their Children to Get to Know Their Late Spouse's Country.

Finally, I noticed what appeared to be a catchall category for anyone who didn't fit into the others—the "special extended visa." I dialed the consulate.

"*Buenos días,*" I said to the woman who answered the phone. "I would like a special extended visa. My husband was from Colombia. He died last year and I would like to spend time with my-in-laws."

"Are you retired?" said the voice, who identified herself as María. "We give visas to retirees."

"Oh yes," I answered. "I receive a widow's pension from the U.S. government and I am definitely retired." I was going to fit into one of those categories, somehow.

"Fill out the visa request form, write a letter explaining the purpose of your visit, get your pension certificate apostilled, and bring your passports and your pictures to our office and we will give you a one-year visa," Maria said.

It wasn't easy to prepare the application. An apostille is a kind of international document authentication. But I assembled the papers and took them to Washington in late April. Saúl's sister Eligia told me to do everything early. "When the Colombian government is involved, expect delays," she said.

Eligia must have been mistaken. A few days after I dropped off the paperwork at the consulate, our passports came back with beautifully ornate full-color visas glued into the visa pages of the passports. We were all set.

Except for one thing. The visas were for one year, starting April 30, 2007 and expiring April 29, 2008, and we were going from August through July, to coincide with the school year. I called the consulate in Washington. The line was busy. I was frantic and wanted an answer, so I called the consulate in Boston.

"They gave you visas in Washington without interviewing you to find out the dates of your travel?" the Boston consulate asked incredulously. "That is very improper and unfortunate."

"Yes, I'm sure it is. So what is my next step?"

"I really don't know."

"You don't know?" I asked.

"Well, I would keep trying Washington to see if they can fix it."

I hung up and redialed Washington. After repeated attempts, the call finally went through and I asked for "Pedro," the young man who had taken my paperwork the day I was there. I told him about the wrong dates. "Oh, don't worry about that," he said. "That will be easy to fix in Colombia."

I was starting to see things Eligia's way. I knew in my heart that there was no such thing as an "easy fix" in Colombia.

"Please, there's still time, let me get the passports back to you now so we can get the correct dates," I pleaded.

Pedro was firm.

"No, we cannot change the visas now," he said. "You will fix it there."

Maybe Pedro was right, and we could easily get an extension once we were there. Or maybe I wouldn't need an extension if I found I couldn't hack it down there. I'm not sure I believed any of this, but it was simpler to put it out of my mind for the moment.

Other problems were easier to solve. Friends from Saúl's old job at the Mennonite Central Committee found renters for my house—a missionary couple, just back from 16 years in Afghanistan.

Arrangements on the other end were coming along nicely too. Gloria had spotted a moving van pulling up to a neighbor's home. A fellow teacher had decided to go through with a transfer to another school district, so Gloria ran right over and persuaded the teacher to lease the house to her.

A few weeks before we left Akron, we held a garage sale for all the old clothes and toys we no longer needed. The rest of our stuff went into storage. I tried to fit my cherished KitchenAid mixer into one of the six suitcases, but that would have been a tactical error; not only didn't it fit, it would have given the boys more ammunition for teasing me. I could see it now: whenever I walked the streets of La Mesa, there would be giggling and whispers where I would overhear the word "KitchenAid."

It had been months of details. Now there was this last one, looming large as we stood forlornly outside the airport in Bogotá.

"When did you say they were coming?" asked Mario suspiciously.

"Oh, any moment now," I answered breezily.

I had gotten through the funeral without falling apart. I had made this huge decision to move and gotten the visas—flawed as they were—and packed our stuff and rented the house and delivered the three of us (plus Crystal) safely to this curb in South America. I had laughed off the concerns of friends who said, "Bogotá? Isn't that the place where all the drug dealers live?" Now I wasn't so sure of my capacity to take care of everything, to be everything to my children, to play the role of perfect mother and widow. I couldn't help it that Saúl had contracted a rare form of cancer. I couldn't help it that my children were without a father. But it was my fault that we were stranded on a sidewalk in a city known mainly for its drug cartels.

A man was running toward us at full speed. Before I could warn the boys to watch out for the purse snatcher, Gabriel's face lit up with happiness.

"It's Sergio!" Gabriel called as the purse snatcher morphed into the familiar, sinewy form of my brother-in-law.

Sergio is one of those people who can do anything. The summer before, during a long visit with us in the States, he built a small, artificial-turf soccer field in our basement. Now he was doing something better—saving me from breaking down in front of my children.

"You're here already?" Sergio cried, wearing a big smile and a cap over his bald head. "I didn't think you were coming until later!"

I smiled sheepishly.

Sergio had taken the bus to the airport because Saúl's older brother, Edilberto, was on his way with the truck.

"He should be here already," said Sergio, scanning the parking lot across the street from the airport.

"Why don't you see if you can get some pesos over there?" Mario suggested. There was an ATM at the end of the airport sidewalk.

"Good idea," I said.

I keyed in my PIN and waited anxiously. My plan for the year was to take advantage of Colombia's lower costs and survive on our Social Security benefits and whatever freelance writing income I could generate. The machine whirred as it counted the bills. "Hallelujah!" I cried as I removed 200,000 pesos, the equivalent of $100.

It was another hour on the curb before Edilberto arrived with his small white twin-cab pickup. Edilberto was wearing jeans and a button-down shirt for this trip to the countryside. They had the correct information about the flight, but had assumed it would be delayed as is the custom. At 62, Edilberto had just retired as an engineer for the city of Bogotá. He looks much like Saúl, but his nose and lips are thinner and he does not have Saúl's high cheekbones and thick hair.

"That is a lot of luggage!" he said, scanning the mountain atop the porter's cart. "When I heard six suitcases, I imagined six *little* suitcases."

The two men piled our six over-sized suitcases onto the truck bed. Sergio, Gabriel, Mario and Crystal squeezed into the back seat; I sat up front.

"Can we go straight to La Mesa?" I asked Edilberto, trying to mask my exhaustion politely.

"Of course," he said, pulling out into the heavy Bogotá traffic.

As the truck crept along, Crystal stood on Mario's lap, anxiously checking the unfamiliar air for possible threats to her cherished family's security. Her toenails dug into Mario's thighs amid the jostling of the truck. "Grab her collar and make her lie down," I instructed over my shoulder, just in time, too, because once Edilberto had skillfully negotiated the crowded streets and we were finally out in the country, he gunned it, and Crystal's toenails would have been like spears. We raced past cattle ranches and the tall trees of the high plane around Bogotá. We whipped across a high desert area with what looked like a limestone quarry to the north. As we began the descent toward La Mesa, the truck slalomed through the switchbacks leading down the fog-drenched mountains. Edilberto only seemed to recall that the truck came with a set of brakes when the fog, nature's traffic light, finally spilled into the road.

After the white-knuckled ride, the terrain leveled out and we could see farms growing coffee beans, bananas and citrus fruit. The air turned warmer; at about 1,300 meters above sea level, La Mesa is much warmer than Bogotá.

We passed through downtown La Mesa. The moment we turned off the highway toward our new neighborhood, the pickup truck began bouncing and crashing in the holes in the dirt.

"They never paved this road?" I asked. Funny, I didn't remember that little detail from the last visit.

"Mom, look, I remember that army base," Gabriel said as we passed the entrance to the small army camp that sits on the southern side of Comfenalco.

The truck jostled its way past the rocky pasture bordering the neighborhood and turned into the narrow streets of the dense development where we would live. The houses were uniformly constructed, each with white stucco front and large, brick-trimmed windows upstairs and downstairs. The roofs were green tile, although some owners had built patios or laundry rooms on impromptu third floors. Many of the houses had flowering bushes in the planters between the sidewalk and the narrow street. Small lawns and children's playgrounds were scattered here and there. Pride of ownership was evident in homes where sidewalks were covered with elegant tile and the bricks around the windows were lacquered to a high gloss. But maintenance problems abounded. The street that wound its way in a large circle around the neighborhood won the prize for potholes, and there were areas where the grass had clearly not been cut in weeks.

Edilberto homed in on one of the few parking spaces and brought the truck to a halt.

Gloria, Saúl's sister, dashed joyfully from her house to greet us, her shoulder-length brown hair tied in a ponytail, her huge grin revealing that dental care had taken second place to teaching rural children during her long career as a *profesora*.

"What a miracle!" she cried, grabbing us all in hugs and mussing her nephews' hair. At five feet, four inches, she stood head to head with Gabriel. "I can't believe how big these boys have grown!"

Gloria was close to 60, but she spoke with the urgency of an 18-year-old. In the spirit of her enthusiasm, we skipped a chance to rest up from the trip and immediately trooped over to see the house she had rented for us a few doors away. Gloria unlocked the metal door and pushed it open like the gates to a wonderland.

The first thing that struck me was the living room floor: The 18-inch tan and brown tiles gleamed. Gloria had furnished the orange-painted living area with her old wooden sofa, two wooden chairs and wicker end table. The furniture appeared to have been reupholstered by hand in a thick orange fabric decorated with white and green flowers. She had put a small white plastic table with four white plastic chairs in the green dining area. The door to the bathroom and the six kitchen cabinets were of a handsome dark wood; they appeared to be a Colombian version of cherry. The first floor also had a nicely-tiled bathroom and a tiny kitchen, although there was no refrigerator or stove. A second metal door in the kitchen, opened onto a small patio for washing and drying laundry.

Upstairs were three miniature bedrooms and a cramped bathroom with a plastic shower curtain for a door. The teacher who had owned the house had painted Colombian landscapes directly onto the cement walls. There were lovely tan tiles in the bedrooms and white tiles in the bathrooms.

And best of all was the location. The front door opened directly onto the neighborhood's multi-sport court.

"I'm sorry about the appliances, but here they say that all you get for your rent is the walls," said Gloria.

"It's great, Gloria. Thank you so much for finding it for us," I said. "How much does it cost again?"

"You have to go to the bank and put 300,000 pesos in the owner's account every month. That's about 150 American dollars," the equivalent of my electric bill back home.

We hauled the six suitcases inside and began to unpack. Meanwhile, some kind of drumbeat was going on throughout the neighborhood: *Americans were moving into No. 36-06!* Within minutes, there were children with expressions of polite curiosity peering through our black-trimmed windows. Mario and Gabriel stayed inside, shyly.

Finally, one of the children—he turned out to be our next-door neighbor Carlos—took the initiative of actually knocking on the half-open door.

"*You want play soccer?*" he asked in his best schoolboy English.

That was all that was needed. Gabriel and Mario flew—practically knocking me over as they ran out the door. There was a flurry of excited activity, and soon they were choosing teams. Mario got the ball, dribbled down the field and scored the first goal. An hour later Gabriel and Mario each had a handful of new friends.

That night Gabriel and Mario slept in the bunk beds Gloria had left in one of the bedrooms. I slept on a thin cushion on the floor next to them. As we settled down, we discussed the schools we planned to visit the next day.

"I need to pick a school based on three things," said Gabriel. "And those are?" I asked, bemused.

"Number one is sports," he said confidently. "I want to play soccer every day."

"Okay," I murmured, beginning to doze off. "Number two?"

"Number two is what time do I have to get up in the morning."

"Good thinking."

"And the third is …" Gabriel's voice trailed off.

"I hope it's academics," I said with mock sternness.

"What's academics?" asked Mario.

Two

GOATS AND ACADEMICS

In daily life [at the American Mennonite School of Cachipay in the 1960s], we learned the concepts of heaven, earth and hell, which was a behavioral structure that somebody at that school had invented. At the end of the year, those who stayed in heaven the whole time got a trip to the capital—as tourists. I only stayed in heaven one year and got to go on that trip. The other years were a delirious trip between earth and hell until one day I became resigned to feeling more comfortable under the infernal heat than any other place.
From Saúl Murcia's 2004 letter

Before worrying about all the other myriad details of starting life in Colombia, I wanted to get the boys into school. It was only mid-August, but the Colombian school year starts in February and ends in November. The sooner Gabriel and Mario were squared away with the educational system, the sooner I could concentrate on the household.

It was the afternoon of our first full day in Colombia and we all piled back into Edilberto's nerve-jangling pickup truck to look at the list of schools Gloria had recommended. Gloria taught middle- and high-school social studies, ethics and religion at the big public school in La Mesa.

"You are welcome to consider my school," she said as Edilberto drove to the first stop on our mini-tour. "We have much to offer. But since it's a public school, I thought you should know that we also have some really wild kids."

There were three schools on the list. We tried the two private country schools, but they had already let out for the day and there was no one around to tell us much.

"Okay," I sighed. "We'll try again in the morning."

The third stop was in downtown La Mesa. Again, Edilberto had a knack for finding an elusive parking place on the street.

To get to the American Mennonite School, we had to walk past the Mennonite Church of La Mesa. My heart pounded, remembering how Saúl's connections to the early Mennonite missionaries in Colombia had changed his life. In 1945, Mary Hope and Gerald Stucky were Mennonite missionaries from the U.S. who opened a boarding school—the American Mennonite School—in Cachipay, a small town near La Mesa. The boarding school was for children of the residents of a leper colony in Agua de Dios, about 40 miles south. The Stuckys allowed the Murcia children to attend; they were lepers, too, in a way. Saúl's older brother and sisters were hounded at the Catholic-dominated public schools for being Protestant and refusing to make the sign of the cross or take part in other rituals required by the school priests.

When Gabriel was still a baby, Saúl and I visited Mary Hope Stucky in her airy Bogotá apartment. It was a few years after her husband died, and she had since retired as a missionary. She had to be around 80, but she was healthy and talkative. She bounced Gabriel on her knee and remembered old times at the boarding school, recalling how she and her husband felt it was important to serve an embattled minority, despite the good health of their parents.

"Well, we made room for the Protestant children," she said, chuckling at her little bit of rule bending. Mennonites can get sanctimonious, but I can hardly think of anything more worthwhile than running a boarding school for needy children in war-torn rural Colombia, and making exceptions to the rules to reach out to others in need.

Despite the Stuckys' offer to educate the Murcia children, Saúl's father (whose name was also Saúl) did not want to send his youngest son to a school of any kind. The father of eight only had a few years of formal education himself and figured he'd gotten by just fine. Also, he needed help on the farm. "Sending three of them to school at a time is plenty," he would say.

Saúl never talked about this aspect of his father's stubbornness. He only mentioned once that he didn't start school until he was 9. And I didn't know until I read his letters that it was his father who insisted on keeping him home, first to herd dairy cows on unfenced pasture in Cajicá, where his father managed a farm, then to help in marathon sessions of milling sugar cane after the Murcias bought their own land near La Mesa. In one of the long letters Saúl wrote to his siblings and cousins after his first cancer surgery, he recalled their childhood together and argued for remaining connected to Colombia despite the seemingly intractable problems of poverty and violence. In one particularly poignant passage, he described how he had desperately wanted to learn how to read and write, and how his parents had argued and argued over it.

"My father saw the reality of his daily challenge of trying to produce enough for the family's survival," Saúl wrote. "It was the theme of conflict during their breaks and whenever they noticed that I was growing older, without school and without hope."

It was Flor, Saúl's mother, who finally changed his father's stance. The Mennonite boarding school that changed Saúl's life was just 14 miles down the road from the America Mennonite school where I was now taking my boys.

"We learned the importance of being good boys and girls, of always looking for the good in everybody and always taking care of the neighbors," wrote Saúl. "The other great thing about the Mennonite School was that was where I fell hopelessly and permanently in love with soccer, this sport which gave me the structure of running with a purpose, the chance to compare my life with a game and be part of a team."

I was awash in these thoughts as I shook the hand of Guillermo Vargas, the principal at the American Mennonite School—or Colegio Americano, as it was called. I had e-mailed him previously to find out about the school's requirements.

"So you finally made it," he said. "Do you realize I studied at the Mennonite school in Cachipay with Saúl's brother and sisters?"

I wondered if Guillermo's parents were from the leper colony, or whether he had also been admitted under the Protestant exception. As blunt as I can be, I couldn't find a suitable way to phrase the question.

The sounds of students talking and playing echoed throughout the crowded cement blue and white building. Gabriel had already made me promise not to tell anyone he needed help with Spanish. He had heard enough about the school's options and had already talked with the neighborhood kids about this school. He had mentally checked off his three educational prerequisites and was left with only one question.

"Can I start tomorrow?" he asked.

"Why, yes," the director said. "You can attend for free this fall, and then officially matriculate in January. Now you have to go get a haircut and buy the uniform. Students here are expected to have short hair, clean clothes and polished shoes."

We bought the uniform at the school store and then walked around until we found a little beauty salon.

"He needs his hair cut for the Colegio Americano," I said to the stylist. She grabbed a heavy pair of clippers like a homesteader reaching for a rifle, and fastened the ammo clip: an attachment that was sure to leave Gabriel nearly bald.

There was a look of horror on Gabriel's face. We had been arguing for the last few years about his hair, the same argument that was probably playing out in the homes of every preteen boy in every country. He wanted it long and ragged; I wanted it short and neat.

But, as much as I wanted to prevail in our age-old argument, I didn't want it at the expense of traumatizing my child. "Excuse me," I interceded, just as the stylist was going in for the kill. "Can you trim it a bit with the scissors instead?"

Gabriel shot me a broadly grateful smile, the kind every mother hopes for. It was worth losing the argument.

The next morning Gloria took the newly shorn but not embarrassingly so Gabriel to the American Mennonite School. Mario and I stayed in to have breakfast and then went with Gloria to look at the two country schools from the previous afternoon. We thought these would be better for

Mario in fourth grade than the overcrowded and loud American Mennonite School.

The first country school—The Divine Child—was almost too country. Chickens and goats meandered across the schoolyard in a never-ending recess period. Carlos, the boy next door who was the first of the children to knock at our door, was a student there and was delighted to see Mario.

"The teacher we have for the next three hours doesn't even teach us anything!" he crowed. "You should stay and we can just play all morning!"

That didn't win me over. Nevertheless, Carlos dragged us to meet the teacher who didn't teach, a young man in blue jeans, T-shirt, and a vacant expression. Gloria frowned.

"Do you have a college degree?" she asked without preamble.

"Oh yes, in computers," he answered with a mildly stoned look on his face.

We had seen enough. I called Mario away from his friends and we walked to the gate of Divine Child to wait for a taxi. The physical education teacher was at the gate as well, picking up a student.

"Does that computer teacher really have a college degree?" I asked.

"No, just a high-school degree and a technical certificate," the gym teacher answered cheerfully.

Gloria was fuming. "I am so disappointed in how that school has deteriorated," she said when we were out of earshot of the affable gym teacher.

We took a taxi to the Liceo Campestre, a newer school sitting next to an abandoned hacienda on a hill above La Mesa. The principal showed us around the brightly colored classrooms and cafeteria. Then she took us to the soccer field and pointed out the path leading to the swimming pool. She introduced us to a few teachers and explained that the school day went from 8 a.m. to 1 p.m., with optional afternoon classes in music, English, soccer and swimming. Gloria asked about the religious education.

"We are Catholics but not dogmatic about it," said the principal.

Gloria and I were excited on the way home, but Mario wasn't feeling the love. "I want to go to Divine Child!" he insisted. "I have more friends there, and they all say they like it!"

"Of course they like it, there are no academics," I said.

"Oh. Academics again," Mario pouted.

"Sweetie, the Liceo Campestre looks a lot more organized, and I didn't notice any spaced-out teachers there," I said. "Or loose goats, for that matter."

Because we had not yet located the driver of his school bus, we took a taxi to pick up Gabriel after his first day of school. We waited by the gate as the students streamed out. A girl came right up to me, glancing sideways as if she were the advance person for a rock star's security entourage. "He'll be here in about 30 seconds," she whispered.

I thanked her and looked up to see Gabriel making his way toward the gate, surrounded by a crowd of admiring students. I waited until after the rock star had dismissed his entourage before daring to address his worthiness.

"Aside from clearly making a lot of friends, how was your day?" I asked, hoping to hear some actual details about my oldest child's first day of school in Colombia.

"What? Oh, fine," Gabriel said. "Listen, I have to be at the main sports park at three o'clock for soccer."

"Wonderful," I said, looking at my watch. "That gives us 45 minutes to get home, eat lunch and find this sports park."

The sun was shining brightly as the three of us headed to the bus stop to take Gabriel to his pickup game. We finally saw the bus driver and flagged him down. Mario and Gabriel were ready to jump in, but I had to go up to the windshield first and check the sign.

"What are you doing, Mom?" Gabriel asked me in the voice that says, "This is too embarrassing for words."

"I was just making sure it was the right bus," I answered dimly.

"Oh mom," Gabriel groaned. "There's only one bus through our neighborhood, Route Number 1."

It was only our second full day in Colombia; how did he know that? And to think I had been worried about how the boys would adapt.

A fellow passenger told us where to get off for the sports park.

"This is like mugger's alley," Mario said dubiously as we headed down a strangely quiet street.

"Don't be silly," I said, noticing some anti-paramilitary graffiti on a wall.

We arrived at the park unscathed.

"Okay, now you need to leave me here alone, Mom," said Gabriel.

"Uhh … I don't even know this neighborhood or the friends you're meeting," I said. "After I meet them, maybe Mario and I can take a walk."

To Gabriel's horror, I went right up and introduced myself to the 12-year-old boys on the small cement soccer field. Then, true to my word, I took Mario for a walk down the main highway that passed the park and led into town. On the way, we stopped at a furniture store and then went for ice cream cones. Sure that we had given Gabriel enough space, we trudged back to the park.

"Mario, do you want to play?" called a tow-headed boy who looked like Mario's twin. Mario detached himself from me with scary alacrity, leaving me to bask in the sun and in the wonder of how quickly and easily my children were finding their way.

Maybe I should not have been so surprised; perhaps Saúl had laid the groundwork for his children's easy adaptation to Colombia. We went to Colombia soon after our wedding in 1989, and almost every two years after that. On one trip the airline personnel were even a little critical of us. Mario was six weeks old and Gabriel was 23 months. Under the airlines' rules, they could both travel for free, which seemed like a good enough reason to go.

"Does your doctor know you are doing this?" the attendant asked when we checked our luggage.

"Yes," I said firmly, without adding that the doctor had also questioned me about the wisdom of taking such a young infant so far. I *was* nervous about taking my babies to Colombia, but it was none of the attendant's business.

As soon as we got on the plane, Saúl smiled and pointed to two seats in first class. "What?" I said. As a surprise for me, Saúl had used his frequent flyer miles to upgrade our seats from coach.

As soon as the plane took off Gabriel fell asleep, snuggled peacefully on his father's chest. Mario was wide awake. I nursed him and sang to him and worked hard at keeping him happy. After about two hours, Gabriel woke up. He also wanted to be entertained.

"Why don't we try switching?" Saúl asked.

Saúl had had a good nap and I was tired, but Gabriel wanted to change places with his brother so I agreed. Almost as soon as I handed Mario over, he went to sleep on Saúl's chest, and Saúl also dozed off peacefully.

By then I was tired, but Gabriel had had a nice nap and needed at lot of attention—even first class was cramped for an active almost two-year-old. We ate snacks, read books and played games for hours. Finally the plane landed waking Saúl and Mario from their long nap.

"That was easy, wasn't it?" he said.

"Good shot!" I yelled as Gabriel deftly whipped the ball into the goal.

Then it was back through Mugger's Alley to the bus stop.

"Mom, here comes our bus," Mario said. I have good vision, but I could not yet read the sign on the approaching bus.

"How can you tell it's the right one?"

"I don't know," said Mario. "I just can."

Maybe we were going to be okay after all.

Three

THE BOMBING

While my parents dedicated themselves to cultivating a rocky patch we dared to call the Good Luck Farm, trying to make it produce something to eat or to sell at the market, I spent my adolescent years living and studying with my four sisters (and occasional visits from my mother and my other sister) in one room in the city of Facatativá. The house was big and we could cook in another room, but the space was limited. These were times in which we had to convince ourselves, without doubt, that we would be able to one day escape the misery and the hunger and be productive members of Colombian society.
From Saúl Murcia's 2004 letter

*A*s Gloria showed us around our house, she kept coming back to the same point: conserve water. "They only bomb on Wednesdays and Saturdays," she said. "There's bombing?" I asked in alarm. Gloria had promised that La Mesa was a safe part of Colombia.

The word for pumping in Spanish is *bombear,* which sounds an awful like bombing. But all it means is pumping. In our neighborhood, water flowed from the city water main into a large underground storage tank. On Wednesday and Saturday nights, if the tank was full, the water was pumped up into the 250-gallon black plastic tanks each house has on its rooftop. Water from the

23

rooftop tank flows into the plumbing around the clock, but the 250-gallon tank will run out quickly if it's not conserved carefully. Residents take advantage of the "bombing" to wash clothes and do anything else that requires a lot of water, because any water used during a bombing does not count against the 250-gallon allotment.

Probably when some engineer designed the system 15 years ago, it worked perfectly on paper. But in reality, the city doesn't always send the water, and the person who is supposed to pump twice a week does not always remember to do it. When people run out of water, they borrow from neighbors. If it rains they collect the rainwater using buckets under their downspouts.

As Gloria said over a cup of coffee during my first week: "We have had water problems in this *barrio* for ages. Some people have moved because they got so fed up with the water shortages."

I instituted a new rule in the house. Only flush if absolutely necessary. As a New York politician said during a water shortage in the 1970s: "If it's yellow, let it mellow. If it's brown, flush it down."

On our second day, I was cleaning the kitchen cabinets when I heard Mario flush the downstairs toilet and go back outside to play. "Don't flush!" I yelled too late.

"Don't worry Mom, it was brown!" Mario yelled back as he ran out the door.

I forgot about the flushing incident until about five minutes later, when I realized the toilet was still running. I ran to jiggle the handle and shut it off, wandering how much of our precious 250 gallon allotment had just flowed down the drain. A few minutes later, I had my answer.

"Mom, there's no water," I heard Gabriel call from the bathroom.

"What? But it's only Thursday!" I wailed. There'd be no bombing until Saturday.

Welcome to Colombia.

Luckily, the backup tank in the laundry patio was full. So we could scoop water from that tank into buckets for toilet flushing and bucket showers. The backup tank had only a few inches of water by the time Saturday rolled around. By then, the air fresheners I had purchased were no longer doing the trick.

Early Saturday, pre-bombing, Mario was about to use the upstairs bathroom when he cried, "Uy, I can't stand the smell!" He grabbed a can of air freshener and pressed the nozzle down and held it.

Oh good, now the air reeked of Glade's "Fruit Explosion."

"Oh no Mario!" yelled Gabriel. "I can't stand *that* smell."

"Well I can't stand the smell of a stinky toilet," Mario yelled back.

I waved my arms for peace.

"Mario, just use the can to give a quick sprits," I instructed him.

"Mom," Mario said. "I want water!"

"I know sweetie," I said. "We'll have some again by tonight."

No lovelorn teen ever waited by the phone as anxiously as I waited that Saturday night for the bombing. A few minutes after 8 p.m.—the appointed time—I went outside to find my neighbor checking her water meter.

"Any bombing?" I asked.

"No," she said darkly.

Now you know what neighbors talk about on the sidewalks in Comfenalco.

The next morning I dropped by the neighborhood store, Don Jorge's, to buy milk. Don Jorge is widely liked and respected. He opens at 6 a.m. and closes at 9 p.m. and gives credit to the many cash-strapped families in the neighborhood. Just then he was handing a customer a bucket he had filled from his own tap.

"Appearing at her house with a brick in each hand is not the solution," Don Jorge was saying to the customer. "She was wrong, but there's no reason to throw a fit."

From this I gathered that the woman responsible for turning on the pump had forgotten, and that I was not the only person without water. One sweaty, angry neighbor had appeared at the woman's house and ranted and raved in fury. In turn, the woman who was supposed to turn on the pump responded angrily, saying she was not going to turn the water on at all. But apparently she relented, because after dinner that night we heard excited cries.

"*Bombing!*" a child yelled with urgency as he ran by. Not since Paul Revere's ride was a message so stirring.

"We need to act quickly!" I said. "Mario, go take a quick shower and clean the downstairs toilet. Gabriel: You are in charge of refilling the backup tank and cleaning the upstairs toilet. I'm going to wash some clothes. Quick, to your battle stations!"

I hunched over the little cement stone washing tray—my only means of washing clothes. I had learned how to use these stone washing trays during visits to Saúl's parents' farm. My cement tray, at about 16 by 21 inches, was a little smaller than the one at the farm. The bottom was scored in a herringbone pattern, in order to be able to scrub grime—and dye—off clothes with greater efficiency. I set my khaki Talbots shorts in the tray and threw a bowlful of water from the reserve tank over them. Then I grabbed the blue laundry soap bar and rubbed it all over the shorts. Next I rubbed the shorts up and down over the herring bone scoring, and threw water over them to rinse them out. I have never been all that interested in fashion, but as I hung my shorts on the line, I said to Gabriel as he raced back and forth on water patrol, "I wonder if any Talbots shorts anywhere else in the world have ever been stone washed?"

"Yeah?" he asked, out of breath. "I wonder if my stone-washed jeans have *ever* been stone washed!"

I gave him a look and grabbed his jeans next. I continued like that, as fast as I could, until the clothes were washed.

While I was waiting to get my kitchen set up, we ate at Gloria's. Sometimes I cooked and sometimes she cooked. She was always welcoming and generous with her kitchen, but I figured that the sooner I was out of her hair and cooking and washing on my own the better. Sergio wanted to make it easy for me to equip the house. He called and offered to pick me up and take me shopping in Bogotá. Gloria said she had an easy day at school and she would be able to come home early and watch the boys after school.

I looked around my empty house and tried to picture what I needed to buy. It was an odd feeling. When Saúl and I got married, it did not even occur to us to register at the local department store. I hadn't really thought of what you need to set up a household. We had just acquired things here and there during 16 years of marriage.

There were certain treasures, like my Kitchen Aid mixer and my waffle iron, that I had wanted to bring to Colombia. But I left them at home to avoid going over the suitcase weight limit. Now I needed to figure out what to buy in Bogotá. I couldn't find any paper, so I grabbed a piece of cardboard my printer had been packed in and began making a list: plates and bowls, dish towels, soup pot.

Early the next morning, just after Gabriel and Mario had gotten on their respective school buses, Sergio walked across the soccer field in front of my house carrying an old cardboard box. "Here are some things my wife's friends lent to help you get settled," he said.

"Thank you," I answered, hoping my voice did not reveal my dubious feelings about "some things borrowed from friends."

When I first opened the box, I saw a soup pot that was so ancient and dented it never would have made the cut at my local Salvation Army. It would have gone straight into the trash. It did *not* remind me at all of the glass-lidded stainless steel soup pot I left in storage in Pennsylvania. But beneath the soup pot there was a treasure that surprised me: an old but beautiful chrome-plated Black and Decker waffle iron.

"Thank you!" I said again, but this time I meant it.

The box also contained plates, flatware and a pitcher. I left it on the little white kitchen table Gloria had lent me and climbed into Sergio's maroon Renault sedan. He drove down the dilapidated streets of the barrio and out onto the dirt road that led to the highway. Soon we were racing back up through the mountains that surround the high plane of Bogotá. "We're going to Cafam, which has good selection and good prices," Sergio said.

We parked at a mall that looked surprisingly similar to malls in the United States. On the outside, the only differences were fewer parking spaces, and more security guards and taxis. I pushed the shopping cart up and down the aisles of the elegant store, choosing everything from kitchen towels to silverware.

I felt oddly jittery. The prices in pesos contributed to my unease. The flatware was 29,000 pesos. The dish-washing rags were 2,000 pesos. *Was I spending too much money?* I wondered, unable to do the math in my head. Sergio was helpful and informative, but did little to calm my nerves. "That's a good brand," he said, pointing at a plastic bowl that looked good. "That's a crummy brand," he said, pointing at another one that looked about the same.

Forgetting that I probably could not burn my stone countertop even if I wanted to, I searched on a high shelf for a hot pad. Suddenly one of them came tumbling down, hit the floor, and the little ceramic inset depicting a chubby baker fell out and broke into 20 pieces. A salesman hustled over.

"I'm sorry," I said. "I can pay for it if you wish."

"No *señora*," he said, as he grabbed a broom and a dustpan and began sweeping up the pieces. "Accidents happen."

Finally I pushed the loaded cart to the checkout. The bill was 323,000 pesos. Sergio helped me with the math. "You spent about $160," he said.

"Considering everything I chose, that's pretty good," I said. I was just starting to calm down and feel better when Sergio's cell phone rang. He answered it, but there was nobody there.

Then he received a text message. Call Gloria.

"I'm sorry, Rebecca," Gloria said. It was about 1 p.m. "I got held up at school and Gabriel is home alone. When does Mario get home?"

My unease began to grow into panic, but I took a deep breath. "Mario has after-school soccer until four o'clock," I told Gloria. "I'll be back by then. Can you call Gabriel and make sure he is okay?"

"Yes," she said. "I'm sure he's fine."

Colombia's telecommunications laws appeared to have been written entirely for the companies' benefit. They charged extra to call telephones that are not part of their network. And some calls simply cannot be made. For example, I cannot call cell phones from my land line.

So Sergio and I raced around the mall trying to find a way to call Gloria's house. A security guard thought he knew how to call Gloria's house on his cell phone, but that didn't work. Finally we found a little store in the basement of the mall that sold phone calls—literally.

I stepped into a little booth, dialed Gloria's house, and talked to Gabriel.

"I'm sorry you're there alone," I said. "I'm fine," Gabriel answered, reminding me with his calm voice that he was *twelve* after all. "Gloria and I were just not sure when Mario got home."

"That's fine, then," I said. "We'll leave now and see you in about two hours." "Okay mom."

I hung up the phone and went back into the mall hallway to find Sergio. "*Señora!*" I heard a woman's voice call to me from inside the store. "You forgot to pay."

I turned around and headed back into the store. Luckily she had not called security on this forgetful gringa.

"Sorry," I said. "How much do I owe?"

"One thousand pesos."

I found a one thousand peso bill in my wallet and handed it over. It was hard to get used to the money. But slowly I did the math in my head. A dollar is equal to 2,000 pesos. One thousand is one half of 2,000. So the phone call cost 50 cents.

Sergio and I loaded all the bags into his car and raced back to La Mesa. When we arrived, Gabriel and Mario were playing soccer with their neighborhood friends.

The next morning Sergio and I went to an appliance store and bought a stove. Gloria had already bought herself a new refrigerator and given me her old one. Since I love to bake, I was thrilled to have a stove, but the centigrade markings on the stove dial were confusing. *What in the world is 290 degrees centigrade?* I wondered. Baking has always been my specialty and good baking requires that recipes be followed carefully. I went to the Internet to look up the Fahrenheit translation of the four temperature settings listed on the oven. I carefully copied the Fahrenheit translation in permanent marker next to the temperature settings. Then Sergio showed me how to light the stove. "How well do you think the thermostat functions?" I asked. A properly calibrated thermostat, which keeps the oven at the set temperature, is key to good baking.

"Thermostat?" Sergio laughed. "This is a Colombian oven. You have hot, very hot, and very, very hot."

"That's why Colombians love their bakeries so much," I said. "Their ovens don't work properly."

I wondered if I could learn to tell if the temperature was right by putting my hand in the oven, or if I could maybe buy an oven thermometer in Bogotá.

But I had more urgent problems. Mosquitos. Mosquitos had discovered that house 36-06 finally had residents again and they were feasting ravenously. At night, as Gabriel was trying to sleep, they bit him furiously.

"Mom," he called from his room at bed time. "I'm being eaten alive."

I sloshed mosquito repellent on his face and neck, and pulled his covers higher up over his body. Then I went to bed (purchased and delivered by

Edilberto) and pulled my covers up to my nose to keep the mosquitoes away. But apparently I left one hand out. When I woke up my hand was sore from being feasted upon during the night.

Since we were almost a mile above sea level, mosquitoes didn't carry malaria. But they were known to occasionally carry dengue, a flu-like illness that can bring nasty complications.

I went to the market and bought a big mosquito netting for each of us. Gabriel's was baby blue and a little frilly. But the mosquito torment had attenuated his normally acute sense of fashion. "It's great mom," he said as I tied the hoop at the top of the netting to the rafters, and spread the long diaphanous skirt out around his little bed.

Mario's mosquito netting was white and had six strings I used to tie it to the upper bunk.

"This is so cool," he said. "It's like getting to sleep in a tent every night."

I thought of Saúl, who had a calm personality—except in the presence of bugs. Whenever a fly got into our house he would pursue it until he killed it. As he ran around the house with a fly swatter, Gabriel, Mario and I pretended to huddle in fear that the fly would land on our heads and Saúl would be forced to decide between hitting one of us on the head with the fly swatter or letting the fly continue to torment him. As I curled up that night under my new yellow mosquito netting, I thought, Saúl would have bought them on his way from the airport.

Four

Resident Fear

I had only travelled in the "San Vicente Fleet Buses," with passengers squished in up to the ceiling, managing to somehow violate the basic laws of space and mass. Oh and I had also travelled in slightly nicer buses from Facatativá to Bogotá. The problem was never so much the aesthetics or the comfort but rather how to pay for the ticket.
From Saúl Murcia's 2004 letter

As I raced from place to place and from mystery to conundrum during our first few days in Colombia, I did not have time to be afraid. Plus, Sergio and Gloria kept in almost constant contact, so I never felt alone. But the cocoon of constant company and contact had to break at some point. It was the Colombian government that forced the issue.

"You and the children need to be here at 8 a.m. for fingerprinting," an unfriendly official told me when I asked about the registration process for foreigners. "Failure to comply can result in fines and deportation."

The resident alien registration process brought home the reality of our lives. We weren't here for a quick touristy visit. We weren't going to skim along the surface of Colombia the way we had in previous three-week trips. We were planning on living here for a year. And the government, which treated tourists so nicely, had a completely different set of rules for residents. Residents needed to be where the government told them to be, when the government said. They needed identification cards and fingerprints. Sergio knew that I wasn't quite ready for this and wanted to help. "Look," he said. "I'll drive out to La Mesa, pick you up, take you and the boys to Bogotá and then bring you back and drive home." The drive from La Mesa to Bogotá was about two hours. So he was talking about spending more than eight hours at the wheel just to shield us from confronting the reality of Colombia too soon.

It was a generous offer, and I knew Sergio meant it, but I also knew that if we were going to be residents of Colombia we needed to be able to travel on our own.

"You don't need to do all that driving, Sergio," I said. "We'll try to find a comfortable bus. If you'd like to meet us in Bogotá to hold our hands once we get there, that would be great."

I tried to sound like it was not a big deal. But in reality I was scared. When I imagined us living in La Mesa, I had not pictured us riding those terrifyingly fast buses as they raced up the slopes of the Andes to Bogotá. What's more, I had not given much thought to the fact that many governments love tourists, who spend money and then leave, but take a much sterner view toward residents who might potentially use scarce resources—or worse yet—cause problems. Gloria seemed to know that we needed to venture forth on our own, as frightening as it might be.

"When you get near the bus stop, hang on to your luggage," she counseled. "Don't let anybody take it until you are sure you have a seat on the bus. And hold on to your purse on the bus, don't fall asleep or set it on the ground."

We took the 6 a.m. local bus to the town square the next morning, and then walked to the Panaderia Velez, a wonderful bakery that was always packed with customers enjoying their rich macaroons and cakes in the morning. I ordered a cup of coffee and tried to focus my sleepy brain on the task ahead. "Gloria said we need to be careful now," I told Gabriel and Mario as they munched on their snacks. "These bus drivers sometimes grab your luggage to try to get to you to commit to their bus, and then force you to stand in the aisles."

Gabriel looked at me. He had lived in Colombia for a week so he already knew that Gloria often overstated the dangers of everyday situations. "Let's go, Mom," he said. We began walking the one block from the bakery to the corner by the market that served as a bus stop. It was early and the butcher shops that lined the block were still closed.

Suddenly a man was yelling at me. "WHERE IS BOGOTÁ?" he seemed to be saying. He was yelling so loudly and quickly that I could not understand. I stopped, paralyzed, and held my purse and my backpack firmly. I waited for him to repeat himself so I could understand him better.

He shouted at me again. This time I understood.

"ARE YOU GOING TO BOGOTÁ?"

I felt myself becoming unfrozen as Gabriel urged me along.

"Mom, don't worry," Gabriel said. "Let's go."

The man showed us to our seats inside the medium-sized red and blue "San Vicente Fleet" bus. He put me in the right-hand aisle seat just before the back row. Gabriel and Mario quickly grabbed two of the back row seats, their body language showing they thought riding in the back of this bus, which was well-used but not too decrepit, would be fun. I sat down and took a deep breath. This wasn't going to be that hard, I thought. The bus pulled out onto the road to Bogotá, leaving behind the neighborhoods and citrus farms of La Mesa, and heading up toward the mountains that surround Bogotá. Gabriel and Mario took out their hand-held video games and I took out my cell phone to call Sergio and tell him when we would be arriving in Bogotá. As I scrolled through the few contacts on my cell phone, a surprising wave of nausea overcame me. I looked away from the phone and tried to focus on the steep hillsides on the side of the road. But the nausea did not abate. I felt the color go out of my face as my insides churned painfully. I looked back at Gabriel and Mario to see how they were doing. Gabriel had set his video game down on his lap and was looking pale.

"Mom, I feel really sick," he said.

The window seat next to me was empty.

"Why don't you sit here and see if the air will help?" I said.

Gabriel came and sat beside me. We both stared out the window, willing our confused bodies to understand that there was no need for panic. I knew the hairpin turns on the road from La Mesa to Bogotá could induce nausea, but it had never happened to me before. I didn't know what to do, but I knew there was no stopping the bus. I felt the sweat breaking out on my forehead as my body struggled to adapt to the motion on the bus. I realized I should have anticipated this possibility. I used to love roller coasters but in the last few years I had discovered that even some kiddie rides at amusement parks could give me an uncomfortable bellyache.

"Does anybody have a plastic bag?" I finally yelled in Spanish.

Another passenger knew what to do.

"Helper!" she yelled up to the front of the bus. "Bring a bag back here, please."

A young man wearing the red polo shirt of the bus company hurried back with some small plastic bags.

"We need two," I said, taking them with a mixture of fear and gratitude. I had never vomited my stomach contents into a small plastic bag and it wasn't a skill I was anxious to develop.

I gave one of the bags to Gabriel as he continued staring out the window and breathing in the cool air as it came in the window.

"Are you okay?" I said.

"It's getting a little better," he said.

Finally the acute state of nausea left us both, eliminating the prospect of testing our skills with the little bags. The bus scaled the mountains around Bogotá and began the smoother part of the journey, across the high plain into the city. It rolled to a stop along a curb at the central bus station, a behemoth unlike any bus station I had seen before. It certainly dwarfed the small regional airports at home in Pennsylvania. I followed the crowd as it proceeded slowly into the broad aisles of the bus station. Little restaurants and stores offering fried chicken, candy and other snacks lined the broad hallways. "Stay close," I muttered to my children as I looked around for a place to recover from the ride into the city.

And there, much to our surprise was a most welcome sight.

"Dunkin' Donuts!" Gabriel said excitedly.

We had hardly ever eaten Dunkin' Donuts in the United States, but the sight of such a famous American brand was comforting. We ordered coffee, juice, croissants and donuts and slid into a booth.

"This is so cool," Mario said as he eagerly munched on a glazed donut.

My stomach was calm by then, but I still felt as though I needed to be cautious. I took small bites of my croissant and little sips of coffee. Gradually I felt my strength was returning.

We went out to the taxi stand and gave the driver the address of the Department of Administrative Security, the office that had advised me, under no uncertain terms, that we were to report for fingerprinting as soon as possible.

The taxi pulled up in front of a modern, glass-enclosed building. We went inside and found about 20 people sitting in waiting area, as officials behind counters stamped documents and consulted computer screens. After checking in, we took our seats and waited to be called. As we sat in the crowded waiting area, conversation swirled around me. I overhead a man with an English accent asking about whether an overseas trip would affect his residency status. Two Venezuelans were bemoaning the situation in their country, where rumors were rampant about President Hugo Chavez's plans for the future.

"He's going to require families to double up in houses," a Venezuelan woman muttered to another.

A friendly-looking middle-aged woman called me over to her counter. I turned in our passports, pictures, and the required receipt showing that I had deposited the fee into the department's account.

"Go through there for fingerprinting," a cheerful middle-aged woman said.

We passed through a metal detector to get to the finger-printing area, a smaller room where officials milled around at computer screens and cameras. I watched an official press each of Mario's fingers into the black ink pad and carefully make impressions onto a white card. For some reason, this sight prompted a new surge of anxiety to rumble through my whole body. I began to tremble in that drab office as the cold reality of my decision hit me. *Why in the world was I putting my children through this?*

They had already been through a lot.

In November of 2004, I walked by the five huge posters of the covers of *U.S. World and News Report*, proclaiming Johns Hopkins to be the country's best hospital in the world. I took the elevator up to the neurosurgery floor to find Saúl. "Hola Sweetie," he said, doing his best to greet me. I kissed him and asked how he was doing. He was gradually recovering from having most of the cancer removed from three vertebrae in his spine and titanium rods screwed to his backbone.

"I hate this hospital and I want to go home," Saúl said.

A social worker appeared in the room and asked me to come see her. "We had a meeting and decided that your husband cannot go home. He needs 24-hour care and intensive spinal-cord injury rehabilitation."

I looked at the social worker in horror. *My husband needs to go home!* I thought. But I understood her point. Saúl's legs were still almost completely paralyzed. The neurosurgeon had admitted that his legs appeared to be even weaker than they were before the surgery. I left the hospital to return to Pennsylvania and search for a spinal-cord injury rehabilitation facility. I toured two local hospitals' rehab-facilities, thinking all the time that all Saúl really wanted to do was go home. Neither facility seemed appropriate, so I called a social worker at Hershey Medical Center, which is about 35 minutes from our house. She asked about the cancer in Saúl's lungs. "Well, it's bad, the doctors think he's only got a few months to live," I told her. "Well then why are you looking to place him in spinal-cord rehab? Take him home!" she said to me.

The next day I went back to Johns Hopkins. I tracked down the social worker there and told her what the Hershey social worker had said. "Oh, nobody at the discharge meeting where we decided your husband needed to go to spinal-cord rehab mentioned that your husband's cancer was terminal," she said.

I looked at her. I was at loss for words. I wondered, *if this is the best hospital in the country, what do they do at the other hospitals?* But she redeemed herself. She flew into action and began organizing everything we needed to bring Saúl home. She called home care nurses and therapists. She called a medical equipment company and ordered a bed, a wheel chair and a commode. She called an ambulance, and got the doctor's approval—all with the speed and efficiency that you would expect at the best hospital in the country.

Saúl was strapped into a gurney and placed in an ambulance, where I sat by his side. The driver answered her cell phone as she pulled out of the hospital's parking area. She continued to talk on her cell phone for the entire 90-minute trip, which didn't bother me too much. But when a dispatcher called her on the radio and she began to drive with her elbows while simultaneously talking on the radio and the phone, I watched with a little worry. But finally, we were home. The paramedics pushed Saúl's gurney up the ramp my family had built and lifted him into the hospital bed.

The next few weeks were a blur of bed pans, physical and occupational therapy, and a constant flow of professionals with varying degrees of professionalism and helpers from our church, who cleaned the house, brought meals, and even slept on the floor next to Saúl so I could sleep in my bed.

Strictly speaking, we should have called hospice and admitted the reality of the situation. But Saúl still had a lot of fight in him. We went to see an alternative doctor who, according to local legend, had cured people with incurable illnesses. The doctor, a trim, fit 50-something with gray hair and a gray beard, sat down with Saúl and asked him about his childhood in Colombia, his diet, and his attitude toward his illness. He did it all with genuine concern, curiosity and a sense of humor.

"Did you eat any game while you were growing up in Colombia?" he asked Saúl.

"Yes, of course," Saúl answered. I was a little surprised. In 16 years of marriage, Saúl had never mentioned eating game as a child.

After the long interview and examination, the doctor said he had hope. "You need to change your diet and speed up your metabolism by eating lots of organic protein and fewer carbohydrates," he said. "I think we can beat this."

As we drove away, clutching a long list of the Amish farmers who sold organic beef, butter and milk, Saúl was more animated and cheerful than usual. We decided to go find these farmers immediately. The next day, we sat down to eat our wild salmon, purchased—much to our surprise—from an Amish farmer, with organic vegetables. "Why are we changing our diet to organic?" Gabriel asked. I was about to launch into a long tedious explanation about what the doctor thought, when Saúl beat me to the punch.

"It's better!" he said.

After a few weeks of taking the alternative doctor's supplements and eating only organic cereal for breakfast and organic meat and vegetables for lunch and dinner, we went back to his office. This time, Gabriel and Mario were with me, so the doctor met with Saúl alone while we waited in the lobby. The boys and I had a habit of playing hangman when we were stuck in waiting rooms, so Gabriel pulled out a pencil and paper. He drew the conventional frame that holds the noose and then five spaces underneath for the word I had to guess. I started with the most common vowel, "E," and the hangman gained a head. I guessed "A" and the A went into the third of the five spots. I starting trying to think of consonants, but none of them was correct and I was losing badly. The hangman grew arms and legs and began to develop facial features. Finally, I got lucky with C and K in the fourth and fifth spots. That's when I realized what Gabriel, in his nine-year-old wisdom, had in mind. Q-U-A-C-K.

One day I served Saúl dinner and then noticed that instead of eating, he was simply crying. He could no longer lift his fork to his mouth. That was when it became my job to feed him.

We spent an afternoon watching old videos of Gabriel and Mario when they were babies. Saúl used to film himself playing peek-a-boo with Gabriel and Mario. For a while, we all enjoyed these funny little movies. We finished watching the moves and it was time for dinner. We started eating, with me feeding Saúl and myself at the same time, which took some hustle with two forks.

Gabriel and Mario began talking about the peek-a-boo video they had watched. One of them asked why peek-a-boo was so interesting to babies. My mother has always said it is very important for parents to understand child development so that they understand why children do what they do at different ages. I saw the children's curiosity as a good chance to teach them something about child development. I launched into an explanation of object permanence. "Babies *believe* that if they can't see something, then it no longer exists," I was saying. Gabriel and Mario were very interested and as we were talking, I completely forgot that poor Saúl was counting on me to fork his dinner into his mouth. We kept talking for a few minutes with Saúl listening quietly. Finally, he chimed in: "I *believe* there are still some potatoes on my plate."

Saúl did not want to be treated by hospice. He could not bear to face the fact that he was going to die. In late April, 2005, Saúl wrote a letter to God, saying that he understood that people wanted him to talk about dying. "Nevertheless, I only want to think and reflect on life, life oh God," he wrote.

"It's as if all my being rejects the idea of wasting time thinking or imagining my death."

Our local pharmacy, however, forced the issue. I went to get yet another prescription for narcotic pain medicine filled and the pharmacist objected. "This is too much oxycontin," she said. "Your husband needs to be cared for by hospice."

I had always heard how great hospice was, but the first nurse that came out had an odd personality. She would sit on the couch with Saúl's pill box, and count pills out loud. Then she would dial her cell phone. "This is Elizabeth from hospice, calling in a prescription for Soil Murcia." When it became clear to me that Saúl could not stand another visit from her, I called the agency and they sent us another nurse.

Saúl woke up on April 28, his 50th birthday, wanting to buy himself an electronic wheelchair. We drove to Lancaster and picked out a fancy model that was small enough to fit into the back of our minivan. "Look Sweetie," he said as he drove his new toy out the front door. I had not realized how tired he was of having to be pushed everywhere. But the thrill of being able to operate the wheel chair was short lived. His right hand became so swollen that he could no longer operate the joy stick.

I hunted around for a solution and found out that a nearby occupational therapist could show us how to bring the swelling down with compression bandages. We went to her and she wrapped Saúl's arm up in layers of cotton and non-elastic compression bandages. He was thrilled when a day or two later he could "drive" again. But the therapist could do nothing about the advancing disease and she despaired as she helped me heave Saúl in and out of our mini-van. His legs were getting so weak that it was beginning to take all my strength to lift him from the wheelchair to the car and back and to the wheel chair.

It was around this time that I dropped him.

Brenda, Saúl's physical therapist, shook her blond head when I had asked her what to do if Saúl ever fell. "You have to call 911," she said. "He is too big for you to pick up and you can't leave him there for long."

Saúl and I both cringed at the thought. Akron is a small southeastern Pennsylvania town with a population of about 4,000 and an all-volunteer fire department that is located around the corner from our three-bedroom semi-detached house. When somebody calls 911, a loud alarm sounds at the fire station, and men who are working locally drop what they are doing and drive their personal cars to the fire station. They change into fire fighter gear and then drive the fire truck down to the scene of the emergency. I sometimes wonder if the city dwellers and newlyweds who pay upwards of a $100 a night to enjoy a quiet weekend in the Lancaster County countryside at one of my street's two bed and breakfasts are warned about our little town's old-fashioned alert system. The sound of the fire alarm at 3 a.m. can be disconcerting to newcomers who sometimes do not understand that it is not a tornado warning or an evacuation alarm. The other characteristic sound on my street is the clip clop of the old order Mennonites' horses as they drive their buggies in and out of town on errands. That sound is much more charming.

When the physical therapist mentioned calling 911, I tried not to think of how embarrassed and horrified Saúl would be if all these local soccer dads and military retirees in their fire gear had to come to our little house to pick him up and put him back in his wheel chair. I focused on correct lifting technique: knees bent, back straight, controlled movements.

For weeks, everything went smoothly. Saúl did fall a few times but I could always lift him onto a step stool, and then back into the wheel chair. But as the cancer advanced, Saúl became weaker and weaker and harder and harder to lift. Saúl and my mother, an occupational therapist with lots of experience in dealing with paralysis, went on the Internet and ordered a transfer disk, a brilliant little piece of technology involving two disks that are attached in the middle. The disk on top is covered with sticky, sand-paper like material to step on. Underneath the top disk of slippery plastic is supposed to slide around on the bottom one, allowing the person who is standing on it to be turned without being lifted completely off his feet. The day the transfer disk arrived, I placed it triumphantly at Saúl's feet as he sat sideways on the edge of the bed. "This should be much easier, now," I said. Saúl smiled enthusiastically in agreement. I fastened the transfer belt around Saúl's waist, bent my knees and did what I had been doing for months, lifting and pulling with all my might to move Saúl to the recliner. Saúl came flying off the bed, swinging around on the transfer disk in almost a complete circle and, as I tried hopelessly to reverse the course, fell slowly on the floor. He lay there in agony. "Go for help!" he said. "I'll see if Barry is home," I said, running out the door.

Barry is a tall, strong, retired factory worker and a National Guard member who is often home during the day, working on one of the many cars in his front yard or building onto his deck. Barry's house is just across a side street from ours. "Barry! Baaaarrrryyyy!" I yelled as I ran to his house. "Saúl fell. Can you come?" Barry came running and we went back into the house. We each grabbed a side of Saúl's belt and heaved him into the chair. "Thank you, Barry," Saúl said. I told Barry about our wonderful new transfer disk. He laughed and said, "You got to be careful with new stuff."

Five

Cooking Without Recipes

The train ride brought back memories of the old train that I used to take from Facatativá to Doima [near Saúl's parents farm], sometimes without money for the ticket, and trying to fool the conductor, or looking for a place to hide so I didn't get thrown off the train in some cold mountain town, like Zipacón, or Sebastopol. One time there were three of us, without money for the ticket and we managed to elude the conductor for almost the whole trip from Facatativá to Doima. He caught us in La Esperanza, one station before Doima, and he was angry and made us get off the train, but we ran and got back on the last wagon when the train started again and the good man was not looking. He caught us again when the train still hadn't arrived at Doima and he said, "You bastards, didn't I tell you to get off? Where are you going?" I did not know what to say. But my friend said, "Please, kind neighbor, we wanted to warm ourselves up in Girardot." The conductor looked at the three of us and said, "Then you are screwed this time, because you are going to get off in Doima." My friend kept it going, and was telling him not to be so mean, that it was the first time they had snuck onto the train, but only to mess with him because there in Doima was where we needed to get off.

From Saúl Murcia's 2004 letter

*G*abriel's bus stopped at the mango tree at the end of our row of houses at 6:35 a.m.—a time when both of us were still struggling to get the cobwebs out of our brains. I set my alarm for 5:45 a.m. and when it went off I got up and staggered downstairs to make coffee. At 6 a.m., I woke up Gabriel. "Good morning sweetie," I said. "There's almost no time to make eggs. Do you want some yogurt from Don Jorge's?"

"I wish I had a Pop-Tart," said Gabriel, staggering to his feet.

"I know what you mean about the Pop-Tart," I said. "I wish I had some Great Grains," Post's pecan- and date-loaded breakfast cereal that had become my favorite in recent years.

At least he did not have to waste time deciding what to wear. At the Colegio Americano, it was the light blue sweat pants with the white v-necked shirt on physical education days and the dark blue slacks and the white button-down shirt the rest of the week.

I put Crystal on her leash and went to Don Jorge's for plain yogurt with Choco Crispies for Gabriel and Mario and a mango yogurt for myself. Soon both boys had eaten and caught their buses. Mario had the luxury of waiting until 7 a.m. for his bus.

A few minutes after they were gone, Gloria invited me over for another cup of coffee with warm goats' milk. I asked her what I should do about getting health insurance. "All our insurance companies are bad," she said between sips of coffee. "And our hospital is terrible. You don't want to go to our hospital if you get sick."

With that anxiety-producing advice running through my mind, I sat down behind the desk of the beautiful young woman who ran the small health insurance office at La Mesa's biggest supermarket, called Colsubsidio. The company is a sort of public-private hybrid that includes a chain of supermarkets, vacation resorts, and a health insurance company. I figured that if I needed to harass them about paying a claim, at least I could do my grocery shopping at the same time.

I explained my situation to the young woman, unable to take my eyes off her perfect olive skin, lovely brown hair and high cheek bones. She narrowed her artfully-made-up eyes at me and said I needed to lie through my teeth to get health insurance.

"Under no circumstances can you admit that you have American benefits," she said. "If you do that you will have to pay way too much for insurance."

I asked how I was expected to pull off this charade.

"Go to the notary office and swear out an affidavit that says you earn the minimum wage here in Colombia," she said. "Bring the affidavit back here and I'll get everything started."

"But I don't want to lie," I protested. I've always been a very honest person. And watching people go to jail for lying to federal authorities during my long stint as a federal court reporter in Texas made me shy of trying to put anything over on any business or government agency.

"It's just a little white lie," she said. "Everybody does it."

Feeling as if I had to make this terrible choice between lying in an official document and getting my children the health care they needed, I walked a few blocks to the notary.

I'm a terrible liar, and I was not even well prepared to tell the lie.

"I need an affidavit saying I make the minimum wage," I told the woman at the front desk.

"What is the minimum wage?" she asked me.

"Uh uh," I hesitated. I knew it was around 400,000 pesos, or $200, but I wasn't sure of the exact number.

She did not seem at all troubled by my ignorance. She asked somebody else for the figure, which was 434,000 pesos a month and showed me where to sign. I paid for the affidavit and went back to the supermarket insurance office.

"So how much will it cost to see a doctor?" I asked after handing over the affidavit and some other documents she had requested.

"One thousand seven hundred pesos," She answered. Not even a dollar.

"What if we need to go the hospital?" I asked again.

"One thousand seven hundred pesos."

"A serious illness, like cancer, that requires expensive treatment?"

"One thousand seven hundred pesos," She answered.

I knew it was too good to be true. And sure enough, over the next few weeks the daily newspaper was filled with reports of a study that showed Colombian children dying of curable cancers because the health insurance companies refused to pay for treatment. I shuddered as I read the stories of parents who had to sue their "health care providers" to get chemotherapy for their ill children. I realized that Gloria was not kidding when she said, "all our health insurance companies are bad."

Politicians love to talk about the efficiency of the market and the power of privatization. But in reality, both in the United States and in Colombia, privatization of health care has resulted in waste, fraud, and the denial of care to people who really need it.

The night after I handed in the affidavit I did not sleep well. I imagined getting a phone call from some Colombian government official who had noticed the discrepancy between the $200 a month I had reported earning when I applied for health insurance and the $2,000 a month I had declared as my income when I applied for my visa. But over the next few weeks, as I anxiously waited for our health insurance cards, I stopped worrying about what the beautiful clerk had called a white lie. After all, I had too many other things to worry about.

For example, what should we eat? The supermarket where I applied for health insurance is just slightly bigger than a typical American convenience store. The produce section was small and not very appealing.

Sergio took me shopping. I told him I knew quite well how to shop by myself, but he insisted that I needed a special introduction to the local art of picking up groceries.

All I needed that day were a few things for chicken soup. At the supermarket, I reached for the dry, white, garlic, which looked just like the garlic in American stores.

"No! Becky!" said Sergio, hastily putting the garlic back. "That is garlic imported from China, which is not good and will ruin the garlic farmers in Colombia." I stepped away from the disreputable garlic.

"We'll stop at the farmers' market on our way home and get some real garlic," Sergio said. I was grateful for Sergio's advice about the supermarket garlic. But I wondered about what other unexpected evils were lying in wait as I tried to get established in this seemingly unknowable country. After we finished buying the chicken soup ingredients, I waited in the car while Sergio went into the farmers' market.

"This is the kind of garlic you need to buy," he said as he handed me the plastic bag containing colorful bunches of fresh purplish and white garlic along with the greens. It did look healthier than the cured, white garlic to which I was accustomed. A day or so later, I ventured into the farmers' market by myself. It occupied La Mesa's entire central plaza. The building had a big warehouse-style roof and large garage-type doors. The floors were dusty old cement and bricks and the stands were tables made of bricks.

"What are you going to buy?" the market stall owners yelled at me. *What indeed?* I wondered. While some of the products were familiar, much was confusing. Bananas were lying around in huge bunches, still attached to the branch on which they grew. The lettuce, which was not neatly trimmed and had been stored at room temperature, looked rotten compared to the neatly arranged supermarket lettuce in the United States. The huge piles of dirty potatoes did not look appetizing. The finger-length white potatoes with black dimples looked good, but I had no idea what to do with them.

After buying some tangerines, an avocado seller called me over. I couldn't resist her large smile and the way she addressed me as if I were royalty.

"My queen," she said. "Do you want an avocado for today or tomorrow?"

"Today," I said.

"This avocado is for today," she said proudly caressing a green avocado that looked just the same as its companions. "But this one is for tomorrow. Why don't you buy one for tomorrow, too?"

I did.

Shopping at the market reminded me of Saúl, and the way he could make something good out of almost anything that was lying around. He never followed recipes; he just cooked delicious meals by taste and instinct. The results were often spectacular: perfectly spiced dishes, deliciously flavored with garlic, onions and cilantro.

One spring day a few months before Saúl died, he tried to show me how to make one of his signature dishes: bacon cheese pasta. It was one of the few dishes that Saúl made that actually had the same delicious taste every time he made it.

Saúl watched from his wheel chair and coached as I fried the bacon bits. "It's got to be really crispy," he said. "Wait until it looks right."

He was trying to teach me to cook by feel.

It was as if he knew that one day I might face a bewildering array of choices in the farmers' market in La Mesa. But unfortunately I had not really picked up Saúl's cook-by-instinct method. I had only brought the latest Mennonite cookbook, a new publication called *Simply in Season*, which focused on using fresh local ingredients. It had some good ideas, but when I was reading a recipe and came to an ingredient such as "one can stewed tomatoes," I felt like throwing the book against the wall. Typical American ingredients like canned beef broth and canned tomatoes were not available at La Mesa's little supermarkets.

I did find everything I needed for *Simply in Season's* lentil rice pilaf. I followed the directions carefully, and served it with a salad made from avocado and cucumber slices. "What in the world is this?" Gabriel said, eyeing my concoction suspiciously. "It is pilaf, which is a mixture of grains, vegetables and spices," I answered, trying to convey my enthusiasm for new dishes.

Gabriel and Mario had become devotees of a neighbor lady's deep-fried empanadas, which were made from corn-based dough wrapped around a spicy potato mixture. She sold them for 800 pesos each, or about 75 cents.

"This is really not good," Gabriel said, after one bite.

"Can we go buy empanadas from Doña Janet?" Mario asked, after his bite.

"No," I answered, with some anger in my voice. "I've worked hard on this dish and you need to try to enjoy it as much as you can."

Gabriel had an idea.

"How about if we eat our pilaf and *then* get an empanada as a reward?" he asked.

"Okay," I sighed. Gabriel's year studying conflict resolution as a peer mediator in sixth grade was paying off.

It was a relief when Gloria invited us over for standard Colombian food: a salad, white rice, grilled beef, fried plantains and cooked vegetables. Gabriel loved everything but the salad.

"Can you make this for us every week?" he asked as he hurriedly forked the white rice into his mouth.

"That would be my pleasure," Gloria answered.

Gloria had installed a small hot water heater in her bathroom. Since our house didn't have one, she invited Gabriel and Mario to take their evening showers at her house.

That night, they both politely refused the offer.

"You are Saúl's children! Of course you don't want to take baths!" she said laughing. "My father used to threaten Saúl, 'If you don't bathe, I'm going to bathe you!' But my mother would spoil him by boiling water for him to entice him into bathing."

I remembered how Saúl used to always joke about taking a shower every week whether he needed it or not. When I would ask him about his supposed reluctance to take a shower, he would say, "The water is very wet."

But in reality he took a daily shower and used a strong anti-dandruff shampoo to keep his chronic dandruff in check. When Gabriel and Mario were little and I was working evenings, he would put them both in the bath tub at once and afterward let them huddle all the way under the covers of the bed until they were warm again.

Then he would pretend he had lost them. "Where are you?" he would call.

When they answered from deep under the covers, he would pretend to be afraid of the talking bed. "The bed is speaking!" he would say in mock surprise.

As we sat there at Gloria's table, remembering Saúl and his eccentricities, it felt terrible that he was gone. But being here—with Gloria and her stories—was a way of somehow staying close to him.

Six

STOMACH ACHES

*The truth is I never knew how the Mennonites got to Colombia. Popular places for
Mennonites in that part of the world were countries like Bolivia, Paraguay, Argentina
or even Mexico, but Colombia, you must be kidding, right? Therefore I always had
trouble explaining to people that my first and second grade teacher, Miss Holda Mayers,
who taught me how to read and write, was from Henderson, Nebraska.*
From a sermon Saúl Murcia gave in 1998

I established a morning routine: I poured boiling water through a small
cloth filter filled with coffee into a large black thermos that was one of
the treasures in Sergio's cardboard box. I heated about half a cup of milk in
the pot, poured that into a large coffee cup, then added the coffee and a little
sugar. It seems like a contradiction, but I've always liked strong coffee with
lots of milk in it.

The thermos was always ready if anyone stopped in for a visit. When
Gloria came by on her way to school, I loved being able to return the favor of
all the cups of coffee and warm goats milk she had served me in my first few
weeks. One morning she knocked on the door as I was drinking coffee and
reading the newspaper.

She was clearly ready for school, with a dressy shirt, nylon slacks and leather shoes. Her hair was combed into a pony tail and she had a subtly but noticeably applied makeup to her high cheekbones.

"It's great to see you!" I said. "Come in."

"Do you have time for a tintico?"

Colombians add the diminutive suffix of endearment to *tinto*, their word for black coffee.

"I need to get on the next bus, but there's probably time," Gloria said.

I took one of the coffee mugs that had come with the set of dishes I had bought in Bogotá and filled it a little more than half way with black coffee. I added sugar and proudly handed the mug to Gloria. She accepted the mug and took an appreciative sip.

"The coffee is very good," she said. "But the cup is all wrong. Here in Colombia we drink our coffee in smaller cups."

I was a little taken aback by her criticizing the size of my coffee cups, but I just nodded in agreement. I thought of what I told my children when they said I served them too much. "You don't have to drink it all if you don't want to."

She polished off the coffee and chatted for a few more minutes before the bus arrived.

I went back to my newspaper and was engrossed in an article about Chiquita, the U.S. banana grower. The company had paid $1.7 million to paramilitary armies who assassinated about 400 Colombian civilians. An American judge was considering whether the negotiated penalty—a $25 million fine and a promise to form an internal ethics committee—was appropriate. "This agreement says that American companies can commit crimes and then buy their way out," the Colombian interior ministry, Carlos Holguín said in the newspaper article.

I grew up with the Chiquita bananas jingle on television. "I'm a Chiquita banana and I'm here to say I'm the best banana in the world today." I knew that American banana growers had long been linked to human rights violations. A college roommate of mine almost cried at the supermarket in 1984 when she thought about the most recent banana-related massacres.

Did American banana consumers have any idea that Chiquita had been implicated in such terrible human rights violations? The phone rang, interrupting my reverie.

It was Mario, calling from school.

"Mommy, my stomach really hurts," he said. "Can you come and get me?"

"Again? I'm sorry sweetie," I told him. "I'll be right there."

Mario's stomach had been hurting on and off since we arrived. But this was the first time he had felt ill enough to ask to come home from school.

I had been taking all the precautions recommended to prevent the notorious *turista* that so often plagues American visitors to Latin America. When it came to eating fruits and vegetables, I followed the adage: "peel it, boil it or forget about it." I even peeled tomatoes, a measure that seemed a little extreme. Many years earlier Saúl had shown me how to dip tomatoes in boiling water for 30 seconds, and then peel them easily while the skin was still hot.

What I didn't know during our first few weeks was that while I was home being very careful to peel tomatoes and boil water, neighborhood boys were treating Gabriel and Mario to ice pops that were sold in the neighborhood for the equivalent of tens cents.

"We call them amoeba pops," Gloria said when she found out the boys had been eating the local ice pops. "At that price, they are probably not even boiling the water to make them."

I found Mario sitting in a chair in the little porch area in front of the principal's office. For a sick child, he seemed surprisingly cheerful.

"The pain comes and goes," he said as we got back into the taxi.

I still did not have my insurance cards so I took him to Dr. Garcia, an independent doctor and a friend of Gloria's, who examined him closely and asked many questions about what he was eating and drinking.

"You cannot drink the tap water here," Dr. Garcia said, as he carefully palpated Mario's abdomen. "The politicians brag that they have improved the quality of the water, but it's still not potable. We all need to boil water before drinking it, even if we've lived here all our lives."

Dr. García said he thought Mario had picked up some intestinal parasites or bacteria. He prescribed antibiotics and a purgative, which is a medicine that makes you feel nauseous as it supposedly cleans the parasites out of your gut. I don't agree with abusing antibiotics or purgatives, whatever they are, but I was willing to try what the doctor ordered. I filled the prescriptions and took Mario home. He relaxed on the couch, feeling mildly nauseous, while the meds took effect.

For about a week after the treatment, he seemed a little better. But then his stomach started hurting again. He also had some episodes of diarrhea. By then I had finally received my insurance cards, so I took him to the clinic above the grocery store.

Dr. Huerta went through the same routine of questions and examinations. "The thing to do is have a fecal sample analyzed so we can find out what's bothering him," he said after he sat back down at his desk. "You need to take a fecal sample to the hospital first thing in the morning."

At the grocery store, I picked up what I needed to collect the sample: a roll of plastic wrap and a little container with its accompanying little scoop. Our shopping finished, Mario and I went outside and saw a taxi that was dropping off a passenger.

"Can you take us to Comfenalco?" I asked.

The driver readily agreed. Once we were in the car I told him that Mario had just finished a doctor's visit because of his stomach aches. "I know about Mario's stomach," he said. "I took you to the other clinic last week."

I had not recognized the friendly driver from the previous week's trips back and forth to the clinic.

"My name is Edgar," he said. "Please write down my number in case you need me again." I already had a few other taxi drivers' numbers in my cell phone, but I agreed.

It had been a long time since I had handled Mario's poop, and I wasn't particularly looking forward to it. When Mario was a baby, Saúl invited some Mennonite church dignitaries to our house in Austin, Texas, for breakfast. I was holding Mario as I frantically mixed crepe batter and served orange juice so Saúl and I could feed his friends a nice breakfast. I felt some moisture on my arm and wondered if it was orange juice or crepe batter. I put a finger in the yellowish spill on my arm, thinking I could taste it and find out what it was. Just before I put my finger in my mouth, I smelled and realized the leaking liquid was neither crepe batter nor orange juice, but baby poop.

Now I tried to remember the best way to catch a stool sample. I placed a piece of plastic wrap inside the toilet. There was no point in letting Mario's poop drop into the toilet water and pick up even more impurities. I got my prize, my little fecal sample, and set the little plastic container on the back of the toilet and went to bed, feeling glad that I would soon know what was causing Mario's stomach problems and how it could be treated.

The next morning I called Edgar, and in addition to agreeing to pick me up, he offered free medical advice.

"Did you keep it in the refrigerator overnight?" Edgar interrogated me.

"Of course not!" I said. "And I don't plan on *ever* keeping stool samples in the refrigerator."

"The laboratory won't accept a stool sample unless it's fresh or refrigerated," Edgar said.

I decided to get a second opinion, and proceeded to the hospital.

I entered a small waiting room at the front of the hospital. Most of the people there were standing in a long line that snaked back and forth in front of a counter where clerks were writing down names and taking payments. "I just need to drop off a fecal sample," I told a security guard who was directing patients right and left.

"Is it fresh?" he asked.

"No, I collected it yesterday."

"Then throw it out and come back tomorrow with a fresh sample."

I couldn't believe it. But I told Edgar he was right and that I needed to try again the next day.

I got lucky the next morning. Mario was able to produce a fresh sample before he went to school. Again I called Edgar and rushed to the hospital as if I were taking an organ transplant by helicopter.

Having investigated the freshness of my son's stool sample, the security guard told me to stand in a long line in front of a counter. If I ever got to the front of the line, the sample wouldn't be fresh anymore.

I went to the end of the line and watched as activity swirled around me. Mothers with small babies were allowed to cut to the front of the line. A doctor appeared and seemed to randomly sign people's papers with a check mark. The line moved ever so slowly. I've always hated lines. When I first got to the University of Massachusetts at Amherst and found out that I needed to stand in lines to add and drop classes, I was furious.

But it had been years since I had stood in long lines with any frequency. Now that I was in Colombia I noticed lots of long lines. People did not use checking accounts very much. Instead they formed long lines to pay bills at banks. There were even people who hired people to stand in lines in their stead.

The security guard told me to have the doctor sign my prescription for a stool sample analysis, which she did without a glance. Finally I got to the head of the line. By then about an hour had passed and I was getting frustrated. "One thousand seven hundred pesos," the clerk said to me. I handed over the money, about 75 cents. "And I have the sample right here," I added helpfully.

"No," he said. "This line is just for signing in. You need to take the sample upstairs to the laboratory."

I wanted to scream, *NOOOOO.* But I forced myself to smile politely and walked up the stairs. The line in front of the laboratory was shorter. When I got to the front I handed the sample to a young woman in a white coat. "Come back tomorrow morning for the results," she said.

The next morning I went straight to the lab where the same clerk handed me the sacred paper I had been hoping would hold all the clues to Mario's illness. But it seemed to say nothing. Under intestinal parasites, everything was blank. Under bacteria, it said, "increased bacterial flora, vegetable remains, and negative for parasites." It also had the word *almidón*. It was a word I knew I should know, but I just couldn't think of what it meant at that moment. I took the paper over to Dr. Huerta at his clinic above the grocery store.

As I sat at in the waiting room, I kept thinking that *almidón* was what was making Mario sick, since I could not remember what *almidón* meant. I asked one of the women who was also waiting to see the doctor, but she said she didn't know. Finally I got in to see Dr. Huerta. "Almidón is like flour," he said.

Of course, *almidón* means starch, I finally remembered. "It seems as though the lab at the hospital didn't find anything," he said, reading the paper.

"So now what should I do?" I asked.

"Well you could try again with a private lab," Dr. Huerta said. "Sometimes they are more careful and find things the hospital lab misses."

"You know Dr. Mora, around the corner from the park?" he asked me. I had been to see Dr. Mora when I first arrived and I needed my blood typed in order to get my identification card.

"Of course, I'll try again with her," I said as I started to head out of his office. "Thank you."

Dr. Mora's laboratory was much easier to deal with. I just walked in a day or so later with yet another of my precious little white containers and paid 5,000 pesos, or the equivalent of $2.50.

But in the afternoon, Dr. Mora was just as mystified as the hospital laboratory. "I went through the sample really carefully," she told me with a smile. "There's absolutely nothing wrong with your child's stomach."

"Then why does it hurt all the time?" I asked.

"He's probably just sensitive to the change," she said. "If you give him a little time, and cut back on his junk food. He'll probably get better."

The next morning Mario was feeling well. It was Saturday so we headed up to the stadium for soccer practice. Mario and Gabriel had joined the town soccer team almost as soon as we arrived and they had both made friends on their teams and were enjoying the practices.

But this morning the children were gathered on the benches at the snack bar with a woman we did not know as well as Raúl, the director of the school.

"I've decided the children should study French for an hour before soccer practice," Raul, told us.

"That sounds like fun," Gabriel said, hurrying away from Mario and me to join the group.

Mario looked as though he might burst into tears.

"What's wrong?" I said, knowing full well that the last thing Mario wanted—or needed—was to sit through a French lesson in Spanish.

"Can you just wait with me at the bleachers?" Mario asked.

"Sure," I said. "Let me just tell the teacher."

I explained Mario's situation to the teacher and then went over to join Mario on the stone bleachers. The teenagers were finishing their practice with a high-spirited game. One small 15-year-old was particularly fun to watch, as he hustled all over his area and controlled the ball with skill and flare.

Mario and I watched for a little while and then I told him I thought we should work on Spanish. "That way the other kids won't think you are over here taking it easy," I said.

"Mom," Mario said. "Do you realize how hard being here is for me? I cannot have a conversation. I just look at people and nod my head."

My heart went out to Mario. In all the excitement over the move, the new house, the new school, and the new soccer team, he had not really admitted how difficult he was finding speaking Spanish.

I was glad the unexpected French lesson gave us a little time to sit and chat. But instead of continuing the pity party, I grabbed a stick and started diagramming verbs in the dirt.

"Look Mario. The hardest verb to conjugate in Spanish is *ser*, which means to be. But you know it's only one of the forms of 'to be.' You use *ser* when you are talking about something permanent: *Yo soy mujer*," I droned on, as Mario feigned interest. "Now let's practice conjugating it in the present: *Yo soy. Tu eres. Él es.*"

I began reviewing the past tense of "ser."

"Mom," Mario said. "That's enough. You're giving me a headache."

Finally the French lesson ended and we abruptly ended the Spanish lesson. Mario hurried away to play soccer with his friends.

Seven

Two Soccer Odysseys

Luisito was my friend from soccer, the sport that had given us a primordial reason to live—and to die if it we got to a point where we had to stop playing. Ironically, it was Luisito who almost lost his life in a game. He was our goalkeeper and an opposing player kicked him so hard in the head that his skull was broken. That year we won the championship, only out of a force of will to have the honor of bringing the trophy to him in his hospital bed, where he endured about six months without anybody knowing if he would walk again. He survived, and he had to leave goalkeeping but he returned to be a starter on the team. He was very tough.

From Saúl Murcia's 2004 letter

*G*abriel was born at 1:07 a.m. on July 14, 1995 at the Brackenridge Hospital in Austin. It was a long, exhausting and often futile labor, started prematurely after my water broke, even though I had no natural contractions. Nurses gave me record amounts of pitocin to induce labor. But as much as the strong, painful contractions forced poor Gabriel's skull against my cervix, the little tube refused to open, resulting in hours of torture for mother, father and unborn baby alike. Saúl later wrote a hysterical account of the two-day ordeal, remembering how I suggested the nurses were former agents of torture for the Argentinean junta, and how he almost got arrested for trying to park the car on the hospital's heliport.

A week later, while the newborn Gabriel and I were still recovering at home and getting to know each other, Saúl went grocery shopping. He passed a yard sale on the way home and saw a small black soccer goal. With a big grin on his face, he carried the goal into the backyard. He clearly could not wait to be a soccer dad.

Saúl's love for the game was infectious. Before our sons were born, we flew to California to see the Colombian national team play in the 1994 World Cup. Saúl tied a Colombian flag, cape style, around his shoulders and cheered loudly for his compatriots. It was not long before I became nearly as enthusiastic about soccer as my husband. In fact, I think Saúl sometimes regretted how badly the soccer bug bit me—especially when I missed church on Sunday mornings to play for my women's team in Austin. But in general, we enjoyed soccer as family, from taking four-year-old Gabriel to his first games at the park in South Austin, to watching the World Cup on television and cheering for our favorite teams and players. When Saúl's cancer invaded his spinal column and made it impossible for him to walk, church friends drove him to an early spring soccer tournament so he could watch the boys play. Mario was only seven that spring, but he was playing on his brother's Under-10 boys' soccer team. "Mario, if you score a goal in this game I'll give you five dollars," Saúl said to Mario as he sat in his wheel chair on the damp grass before one of the games in Wyomissing, Penn. "Pappy, if I score a goal against these big kids, I think you should give me ten dollars," Mario answered.

But our greatest moment together as a soccer family came just a few days before Saúl died. In April Saúl was still able to work, although the cancer had left him paralyzed from the waist down and with little use of his left arm or hand. I noticed that Colombian national soccer team was playing England at the Giants Stadium on May 31.

I called my husband at his office and asked if he wanted to go. He said yes, and I went on line to order tickets, but I found out that handicapped visitors cannot order tickets online. I called Giants stadium and a ticket seller told me she could sell me the tickets, but not send them to me. I told her that sounded like discrimination against people with disabilities. She told me she could send me a letter explaining how the policy of forcing wheel chair users to pick up their tickets at the stadium was not a violation of the Americans with Disabilities Act. By that time, I was annoyed. "What good would you sending me that letter do?" I asked. I went ahead and paid for the tickets anyway.

For the next few weeks, the symptoms of Saúl's advanced cancer grew worse. His legs became weaker and weaker. Swelling in his hands and legs was painful and further limited his mobility. But as his body failed him, Saúl's spirit and will to live grew. We were constantly cooking big meals and entertaining visitors. On April 28, Saúl's 50th birthday, we bought an electric wheel chair and celebrated with a big party at the office and another big party at a friend's farm.

The weekend of the Colombia-England game, my mother, who works as an occupational therapist in Sullivan County, New York, came to help out and go with us. By then we were all excited about the trip. Mario, who was eight at the time, and Gabriel, then nine, made a poster calling for peace in Colombia. They planned to wave it at any television cameras they saw pointing at them. We made reservations at the hotel and asked the reservation person if a recliner could be provided for Saúl, because his pain and paralysis made it impossible for him to sleep in a bed. The person on the phone said that would be no problem and we took his word for it.

The day before the game, Saúl's right leg was swollen as usual, but it was also hot and red. My mother thought that maybe we should cancel the trip. Michelle, our dear hospice nurse, sat on the floor in front of Saúl and diagnosed an infection that would have to be treated with antibiotics. She called a doctor, told him about our travel plans, and persuaded him to let Saúl go on the trip. The next morning we loaded up the car with our bags and then wondered how to get Saúl inside. His feet no longer fit into his old shoes, and we had bought him some large sneakers that had made the transfers even more difficult. His feet would not pivot on their own any more, leaving his legs to twist painfully as we lifted and turned him into the car. My mother improvised a transfer disk—a device that allows paralyzed people's feet to turn when they are being lifted—out of cardboard. It did not work as well as a real transfer disk (which arrived shortly after the trip) but it made it possible to get Saúl into the car. I'm fairly strong but by then Saúl probably weighed 200 pounds and could not help very much.

Once Saúl was in the car, I asked my mother if she had stowed her improvised transfer disk in the back. "Yes, if we lose it we'd have to stop at a dumpster and find some more cardboard to make another one," she cracked back to me. I turned the car toward Reading with my mother driving behind us. Twenty five minutes later, Saúl was in pain. We stopped and turned him outward so he could stretch his legs. We drove on, and did the same thing 20 minutes later. We continued like that all through the 143-mile drive. It took about five hours. Finally we arrived at the hotel. We got Saúl back into his wheel chair and went inside. Almost immediately, Saúl connected with Yulian Anchico, a young member of the Colombian national team. Saúl remembered when Anchico scored a penalty kick against Uruguay to help the Colombian national Under-20 team qualify for the World Cup in 2003. Anchico was obviously pleased that Saúl remembered his moment of glory in Uruguay. We took pictures. We met more players. Many of them took time to talk to Saúl. They signed his jersey and a soccer ball we had brought. Saúl was thrilled. We got back in the car to drive to the stadium. There the nonsensical treatment of the handicapped, which had begun with the staff's refusal to mail us our tickets, continued. We had to pick up our tickets at Gate C, with no nearby handicapped parking. But we could not enter the stadium at Gate C. Handicapped people had to enter at Gate A, a long walk around the stadium from Gate C. My mother, the occupational therapist, was aghast. She noted that Saúl was not too bad off with his electric wheelchair, but that many handicapped people use canes or manual wheelchairs and that the stadium's treatment of handicapped people was really mind-bogglingly shabby.

Finally, we made it to our seats. At least they were good seats. We were behind one of the goals, but we could see fairly well and the upper deck shaded us from the sun. The atmosphere in the stadium was electric, with about 50,000 soccer fans, many of them hard-drinking, vocal, English soccer fans. "Oh, Unfading Glory! O immortal joy. Good germinates in the furrows of pain!" Saúl whispered the lines of the martial-sounding Colombian national anthem, a few tears brimming from his eyes.

The game was great, with one of the players we had met at the hotel, Mario Yepes, scoring one of Colombia's two goals. David Beckham bent in a ball from the right corner that teammate Michael Owen volleyed in, leading to England's three to two victory over Colombia. Saúl was a little disappointed that Colombia lost, but not surprised.

"They played like they never have and lost like they always do," he said with a sad laugh.

We drove back to the hotel, which according to the website, had the latest in handicapped accommodations, exceeding the requirements of the Americans with Disabilities Act. When we got to the room Saúl needed to use the toilet. My mother took the children for a swim in the hotel pool. I looked in dismay at the low toilet seat. I knew I could get Saúl onto it, but how would I ever get him off? We called the hotel operator and asked if they had an attachment for the seat, or a higher toilet anywhere in the building. The response was negative.

Praying that there would be no disasters, I lifted Saúl out of the wheel chair and onto the toilet without a problem. A few minutes later, I used every last ounce of strength to lift him back into the wheelchair. I wheeled him out into the room and we started talking about where and how Saúl would sleep. At home he slept in an electric recliner that we could move and adjust during the night to keep him comfortable. The Sheraton had promised us some kind of recliner, but all they had given us was a sort of couch chair and a foot rest.

As we brainstormed about what to do I burst into tears of exhaustion and desperation. Then Saúl wept a little. We dried our tears, ordered room service and welcomed my mother and the children back to the room. They were thrilled because the Colombian national team had also gone swimming.

We improvised a recliner-type set up with pillows on the couch chair and the leg rest. Somehow, perhaps with the help of the beer Saúl uncustomarily drank with dinner, we got through the night with just occasional adjustments. We had a wonderful breakfast, with lots of cheerful talk with the waiter about the game. Almost the entire Colombian team had left at something like 3 a.m. that morning. But one player, Fabián Vargas, who plays for Boca Juniors in Argentina, was scheduled to fly to Mexico later in the day. We met him while we were checking out and congratulated him for his performance the day before. We wished him good luck in his club's upcoming game in Mexico.

We drove home, delighted with our trip and talking about the future. Maybe we could rent a handicapped van and take a longer trip when the children finished school, Saúl wondered aloud. The euphoria perhaps blinded us a little about the reality of Saúl's health. Saúl lost consciousness and died just a few days later.

Soon after we arrived in La Mesa, the newspaper said the Colombian Under-17 team was playing Nigeria in the Under-17 World Cup in South Korea. The game was at 3 a.m. and would be shown only on cable TV, which we did not have. Gisela, the neighbor who owned a small Internet café around the corner from our house, told me that she could take me to the cable office and that *maybe* we could get cable in time for the game.

Remembering the way Saúl used to follow the Colombian national team obsessively, always signing up for the comprehensive Hispanic packages on satellite television; I stood in the office of the little cable TV company and said, "Can you send somebody out today? There's a soccer game at 3 a.m. tomorrow that I *need* to see."

Sure enough, that afternoon a young man knocked on our door and in about 30 minutes connected our television to one of the many cables stretching around the neighborhood. The next morning I woke up and turned on the television, excited to see the skillful young Colombian players advance in the World Cup. Unfortunately it was not to be. Nigeria was even more skillful, and in a hard-fought 90 minutes, defeated the Colombians two to one. Nigeria was the eventual Under-17 World Champion, after defeating Argentina in the quarter finals, Germany in the semifinals and Spain the World Cup final. My new cable company, unfortunately, did not show any of the games.

When I realized that the senior Colombian national team would play Brazil, the reigning World Champions, in a World Cup qualifying match in Bogotá, I knew we had to be there. I could just picture how happy Saúl would be knowing we had seen such an important game. For weeks before the match, however, the newspaper was filled with stories about how impossible it was to get tickets. "Call Miguel," Gloria said one night at dinner. "He will know what to do."

Miguel was a beloved cousin of Saúl's. They lived near each other in Facatativá while they went to high school and played on the same soccer team. Over the years, while Miguel became a politically connected government administrator in Colombia and Saúl became a church agency administrator in the United States, they kept in touch and remained good friends.

The next day I called Miguel, hesitant to ask him to do the impossible but knowing that it was something he would be willing to do for his favorite cousin's widow.

"The boys and I want to go see Colombia play Brazil," I said to Miguel on his cell phone. "I know the paper is saying there are no tickets available, but I thought you might have a way. I can pay you back."

"Of course we should go," Miguel said. "I'll see if I can get the tickets."

October 15, the day of the game, approached quickly and the demand for tickets continued to escalate. People were arrested in Bogotá for selling fake tickets to the game. Others formed huge lines outside the stadium office, only to be sent away empty handed.

I kept calling Miguel, and he kept telling me that he had not been able to get any tickets. I consoled myself with the thought that I had tried and that watching the game at home in the neighborhood would also be a new experience. The day before the game—a Saturday—we met with Saúl's sister, Flor, and her two children, Samuel and Karen, at the family farm. We waded in the river with Samuel and Karen, and ate potato soup with Saúl's mother. In the afternoon, the jeep driver we had called to take us home arrived.

"Mom, can I stay here until tomorrow? Aunt Flor says she can drop me off at home tomorrow," Gabriel said as we prepared to leave.

"That sounds great," I said, sure that Miguel had never been able to get the tickets.

I kissed Gabriel goodbye and walked up the path to the dirt track where Don Emilio was waiting for us with his red jeep. My cell phone rang.

"Hola Rebecca!" It was Pilar, Miguel's wife. "I just wanted to make sure you were coming tomorrow, since we have the tickets."

"What?" I said. "How did you do the impossible?"

"Very carefully."

I ran back down to the farm house and told Gabriel he had to come home. "Oh Mom," he said. "How come?"

"We're going to the stadium tomorrow to see Brazil play Colombia," I told him.

"But there were no tickets!" Gabriel said.

"I know, but somehow Miguel got them, so hurry, Don Emilio is here," I said.

We ran up the hill and got into the jeep. None of us could believe that we were actually going to the stadium the next day.

The next morning, I threw a few things in a backpack and we got on the bus to Bogotá. We took a taxi to Miguel's house where Pilar greeted us with a big smile and looks of amazement at Gabriel and Mario, who had grown since she last saw them and were now about her height. Miguel arrived a few minutes later and showed us the brightly-colored tickets with the little foil strip proving their authenticity.

"We have to go soon to get in line," he said.

"But the game is not until 4 p.m.," I answered, confused.

A few weeks earlier an usher in a Bogotá movie theater had chastised us for failing to sit in the seats that corresponded to the numbers and letters in our tickets. I did not realize there were assigned seats in Bogotá movie theaters. Soccer stadiums, however, do not have numbered seats.

"You have to get there early or you won't get a seat," Miguel said.

The newspaper said no cameras or food would be allowed into the stadium, so I reluctantly left my camera at Miguel's house. I made sure each of us had a sweater, just in case the sunny morning weather changed, and we headed to the stadium.

When we arrived at the stadium, I was surprised to see that the line stretched for blocks and blocks. But Miguel was not deterred. Showing the diplomatic skills that have helped him during his long career as an administrator in Colombia, Miguel persuaded a boy who was about 14 years old and only about three blocks from the stadium to let us get in line in front of him. Soon the teenager's mother showed up, and Miguel and the mom had an animated conversation. I assumed they knew each other. But they had never met. The mom talked to Miguel because she wanted to ask him to keep an eye on her son. We passed the hours until the stadium opened buying hats, earrings and scarves in the colors of the Colombian flag from the street vendors, reading the newspaper, and talking about the upcoming game. The sun shone brightly and I passed around sun screen to prevent burns. Pilar and her daughter, Ana Maria, brought sub sandwiches around lunchtime and joined us in the line. By then clouds had begun to gather on the horizon. Finally the gates opened, and the people who had been standing so calmly in line suddenly metamorphosed into the bulls of Pamplona, or the horses of the Kentucky Derby. Joining the mob, we dashed as fast as we could to the doors of the stadium and into the stands, claiming our six seats about 20 rows up in the first level of the stadium.

We had barely settled in when a gentle rain began falling, and the game would not begin for another two hours. The stadium was already getting very full, so we did not want to leave our seats. We took turns going back to the hallway under the stands, where there were vendors and bathrooms. We bought plastic bags we could use as improvised rain coats. The temperature, which had been warm and comfortable all day, dropped, and the rain grew harder. Lightning flashed and thunder resonated around the stadium. We really should not be outside in weather like this, I thought. It's not safe. But we did not dare leave our seats. Then hail started falling out of the sky.

"Mom, I need to go inside." Mario, who was lightly dressed in his favorite red windbreaker, was freezing.

I took him back under the stands and sat him down on a dry piece of floor. I took off his soaking wet socks and wrung the water out of them. Then I ripped up one of the plastic bags I had bought and wrapped each foot in a plastic bag, put the sock back over the plastic bag, and put his shoes back on. The day had become more about survival than soccer.

Finally, the rain stopped. Groundskeepers went out onto the field and started poking holes in the turf where there was standing water. Several officials walked to the center of the field with a soccer ball. They dropped the ball from about chest height to see if it would bounce. It did not. As cold as I was, I did not want the game to be cancelled. Despite the soaking wet grass, the officials announced that the game would begin about 20 minutes after the official start time.

Colombians take great pride in their national anthem, and it seemed as though every one of the 48,000 fans present stood to sing along. "Oh, unfading glory! O immortal joy," the chorus went. "Good germinates in the furrows of pain." The stadium seemed to almost shake with the sound.

The Brazilian superstars took the field, led by Ronaldinho and Kaká, whose multi-milllion dollar contracts at the leading European clubs probably earn them more in a week than the entire Colombian national team earns in a year. Brazil has won the World Cup five times, more than any other country. Colombia, meanwhile, has good soccer and good soccer players, but much to the frustration of the legions of Colombian soccer fans, Colombia did not even qualify for the previous World Cups in 2006 and 2002.

So while on paper, it was David against Goliath, on the field it was different. The smaller Colombians played with ambition, teamwork, and speed. The Brazilians played as if they wished they were in much warmer, drier place. Even the legendary Ronaldinho, who has been named the FIFA player of the year twice, allowed a diminutive Colombian defender to steal the ball from him. But despite the Brazilians' apparent lack of ambition and the Colombians' playing their hardest, neither team scored a goal. The match ended in a 0 to 0 tie, which was a huge victory for the Colombian national team and a defeat for the much-favored Brazilians. During the game, the rain started again. By the time it ended, we were all very cold. Gabriel, who had not received the plastic socks treatment I applied to Mario, said he could not feel his toes. We walked out to a street along with the 48,000 other Colombian soccer fans. Of course there were no taxis. We began walking toward Miguel's house. A bus came along, going in the same direction. We flagged it down and got on, relieved that we would soon be home and be able to change into dry clothes. But after the bus had travelled about two blocks, I felt an impact.

"Don't tell me," Miguel said. "The bus crashed."

We got off the bus and stood on the sidewalk while an argument broke out between the bus driver and the owner of the car, which had apparently stopped in the middle of the road with its lights off. Miguel spoke to both men, made sure they had calmed down, and then we walked off into the night again. Before long, a little three-passenger taxi stopped, and all six of us piled in gratefully.

It had been an amazing day, and almost as complicated as the last time I had seen the Colombian national team play.

Eight

VICTOR HUGO

I worked and traveled through many countries on the cruise ship. It was an adventure where I was always coming to a crossroads and trying to decide what to do. It took me four years to realize that I needed to get out of that secure and comfortable life of working, making money, eating well, enjoying life and traveling. One day somebody said we were in Haiti and I decided to get off the boat and visit the island. There the level of poverty was extreme compared to the other islands and once again I faced my own internal war of ideas and I decided one more time that I was on the wrong path—living for myself and contributing to the enjoyment of the rich and wasting food when there were people starving in the world. From there, I ended that adventure and I took the path of an intellectual development, with a lot of doubts, with a lot of fear of whether I could really do it and without knowing how to do it, but I decided to go there and see what I found.

From Saúl Murcia's 2004 letter

Two days had passed since I had washed clothes so there was a small mountain of hand washing to do. I scrubbed at the stains on the collar of Gabriel's white school uniform shirt and hung it up. I continued on to the filthy soccer socks and the underwear. I was thinking I really needed to get a radio to distract me from the drudgery when I heard a knock on the door.

"Mom, the bus driver needs to talk to you. It's urgent!" It was Mario at the door of the house. I stepped away from the soccer socks and hurried over to the bus stop by the mango tree.

Victor Hugo, Mario's bus driver, was sitting in the driver's seat of his little white school bus, smiling at me. "Doña Rebecca, they tried to call you, but they seemed to have your telephone number wrong," he said. "You won *quiñientos mil* pesos in a raffle," he said. Numbers are hard for me in Spanish, especially quiñientos, which means five hundred but doesn't follow the same number convention as the hundreds that precede it. In Spanish, you say two hundred, three hundred, four hundred, and then instead of five hundred, or cinco cientos, you say *quiñientos*, a break in the pattern that is hard to remember and very annoying. So I didn't really understand how much he was talking about. Plus I've never believed in lotteries or raffles. So Victor's news seemed like some stupid joke. I was in no mood for it.

"But I don't buy lottery tickets," I said, crossing my arms in front of my chest. "I don't know what you are talking about."

Victor Hugo hesitated, not knowing what to say.

My neighbor Doña Mercedes was sitting on the bench under the mango tree next to the little playground. As usual, she had her long black hair in a braid down her back and she was wearing her black slip-on sneakers with a skirt. Neighbors sometimes laugh about how Doña Mercedes' almost complete illiteracy makes it hard for her to function in the modern world. She appears to have no income other than occasional small donations from her cash-strapped children. But in this situation, she knew exactly what was going on.

"Señora Rebecca," she smiled, grinning widely and revealing her almost complete lack of teeth. "You bought a raffle ticket from me two weeks ago, remember? And you won a prize! I'm so happy!"

Little by little, I started to remember. I had given Doña Mercedes a thousand pesos (about 50 cents) for the raffle her grandson's child care center was sponsoring. I had done it only because I sympathize with anybody who has to do fundraising and Doña Mercedes had asked me for so little. I had bought the ticket and tossed it in my purse and completely forgotten about it.

As soon as Doña Mercedes reminded me about my ticket, Victor smiled.

"Congratulations," he said. "You have to go to the radio station at 7 a.m. tomorrow to accept the prize."

"Do you still have the ticket?" Doña Mercedes asked.

"No," I answered. "I have no idea what I did with it."

Going to the radio station at 7 a.m. seemed like absurdity upon absurdity. But I got directions to the local radio station. Mario decided that since his school didn't start until a little later, he would accompany me.

We wandered into the building a little ahead of schedule and heard the broadcast being transmitted into a waiting area and a small courtyard. I was hustled into a chair in the transmission booth. Mario followed with a camera.

"Listeners," the announcer said in her smooth-as-silk voice. "We're going to announce the winners of the Enchanted Castle lottery, and we have one of the winners here, Rebecca Murcia, from the United States." The announcer looked at me.

"Buenos días," I said politely.

The announcer looked at me expectantly. I looked back at her, forgetting that the worst thing in radio is silence. Clearly I should have prepared a speech, but this was all new to me. Back home in Akron, bus drivers with the names of weighty literary figures never pulled up in front of my house to tell me I had won thousands of units of the local currency.

"Well, it seems as though Rebecca has nothing to say," the announcer went on.

I have plenty to say about this crazy country, I felt like saying. But I just smiled and murmured in agreement. I was dismissed from the transmission room, accompanied by the president of the Enchanted Castle child care center and its lawyer.

"Now if you can just show me your ticket, we can go back to the Enchanted Castle and give you your prize," the president said to me. "I'm sorry. I lost the ticket," I told her.

After being humiliated on the radio and in front of the playground crowd by the mango tree, I wanted that prize.

She looked at me and at the lawyer.

"We have to give her the prize anyway," the lawyer said.

"Well let's go to the office, then," the president said.

We found a taxi driver to take Mario to school and then walked a few blocks through the rain to the Enchanted Castle child care. The president seemed to be hoping that the lost ticket would be an excuse for her to keep the money. When I saw the children packed into the rundown rooms of the Enchanted Castle child care, I was tempted to tell the director to keep the money and put it toward a playground for the children. All through my childhood, my mother volunteered at Aunt Bessie's Open Door, a child care and after school program serving low-income children in Peekskill, N.Y., a city near where I grew up. I felt as though I was taking money away from a noble cause. On the other hand, I told myself that I had contributed to a successful raffle, and that I would only confuse people if I refused the prize. I sat in a chair in the president's office and thought about my dilemma as the president started counting out a thick wad of bills and stuffing them into an envelope. "Here you are," she said, handing me the envelope.

I thanked her and stuffed the envelope into a purse, instantly realizing that now I faced a new dilemma.

The local radio station had announced that an American woman won five hundred thousand pesos in the Enchanted Castle child care raffle. What if a criminal heard the news and saw me walking down the street?

I walked nervously away from the child care center, more aware of my surroundings than usual and wondering about the best use of the wad of cash in my purse. I hurried to the bus stop at the town plaza. When I got off the bus, Doña Mercedes jumped up from her seat under the mango tree. "Did they give you the money?" she said.

"Yes, and since you sold me the winning ticket, I want you to have this," I said, pulling 50,000 pesos, or ten percent of the prize, out of my purse and giving it to her. "No," she said. "You shouldn't do that."

"I insist," I told her. "I never would have won the prize without you selling me the ticket. So you have to take this."

Doña Mercedes finally agreed, with yet another big smile.

The Internet at my house wasn't working that afternoon, so I stopped by my neighbor Gisela's house. "Congratulations," she said, greeting me. "I heard you won a prize."

"Yes," I said. "I'm trying to decide what to do with the money, and I'm leaning toward buying a washing machine."

"Absolutely," Gisela said. "Don't think about it twice. That's definitely what you should do with that prize."

The next day I decided to take Gisela's advice. Colsubsidio, the supermarket where I bought our health insurance, had a sale on washing machines. I chose a large-capacity Samsung machine with "fuzzy logic" controls.

"I need you to bring it to my house and install it," I told the saleswoman, dimly aware that this American custom for dealing with appliances might not be universal.

"You are asking for installation?" she repeated, looking at me as though I was asking her to do a back flip.

"Yes please," I said.

"I'll go talk to my supervisor."

I could just imagine the conversation taking place in the store's executive offices. "You know that American woman who is always asking why we are out of *salsa picante*?"

"Yes."

"She wants us to bring the washing machine she's buying to her house and install it."

"Well, she's obviously all alone in Colombia. Try to figure out how to help her."

The saleswoman came back and said that the store would install the machine for free but that it would cost $4 to ship it to my house.

The next morning, a truck driver arrived with my new washing machine. "Can I help you with the installation?" I said. I had not handwashed any clothes for the past two days, anticipating the arrival of the machine.

"No, I just brought the machine," he said. "Somebody else is going to install it for you."

A few hours later, the store's friendly security guard knocked on my door. In short order, he had my washing machine installed. I loaded it up, added the detergent, and watched with a new-found fascination as the machine gently agitated the clothes, and then rinsed them and began spinning the water out of the clothes. I had no idea how many gallons were left in my rooftop tank, but

I know the machine used 22 gallons per cycle. I decided to sit down and relax with the newspaper. I was engrossed in yet another article about a scandal within Colombia's privatized health care system. "Doctors can only prescribe medicines if they have not exceeded their limits," the headline said. Suddenly I realized the machine was refilling *again*. Rinsing clothes twice? When water is like liquid gold around here? I couldn't believe it. I started reading the manual to try to figure out how to prevent the machine from rinsing the clothes twice. I could not find a solution. In desperation, I pulled the plug.

Nine

The Whistle Blower

An additional blessing of being at the Mennonite school was that was where I fell hope-
lessly and permanently in love with the sport that has always given me the structure of
running with a purpose, of comparing my life with a game and the chance to be part of
a team.
From Saúl Murcia's 2004 letter

The flyer we designed was straightforward: "Vacation Soccer and English
School. ... Rebecca Murcia invites neighborhood children to practice
soccer and study English beginning Dec. 10..."

The whole idea had come about in the time it took to make breakfast
crepes.

"Don't you guys get an awful lot of vacation?" I asked the boys as I stirred
the eggs and milk into the flour.

"Mom, you knew this was coming. Colombians take a lot of vacations,"
Gabriel said.

"Well, it just seems as if you just had three months off," I said, pouring the
batter into the hot skillet and swirling it around the bottom of the pan the way
Saúl taught me when we were newlyweds. When the sides of the crepe began

to curl inward, I slid the spatula underneath and flipped it. I cooked it until the other side was brown and then put it on a plate for Gabriel.

The boys had enjoyed their summer vacation in Pennsylvania, which started in the beginning of June. In Colombia, they started school in the third week of August. Now it was November and they were about to get another two-month vacation. I made more crepes for Mario and me. I sat down to eat and tried to ignore the way Gabriel covered the top of his crepe with a thick layer of powdered sugar before eating it in huge mouthfuls.

"Okay, but that's a lot of free time," I said, savoring a bite of crepe with a sprinkling of powdered sugar and lemon juice. "What should we do with it?" I asked, completely oblivious to what I was getting myself into.

"We could put on a soccer camp," Gabriel suggested. "That's what we always did back home during the vacation."

Star Soccer Academy, a soccer camp run by the legendary Elizabethtown College soccer coach, Skip Roderick, had been a fixture on our summer calendar ever since we first arrived in Pennsylvania from Texas when Mario was four and Gabriel was six. The week-long camps feature a fun mix of soccer skills, tournaments and break time activities such as trivia contests and talent shows. The coaches are young men and women who either play for local colleges or teach soccer in the area.

Roderick is a former professional soccer player who has coached the men's soccer team at Elizabethtown College in western Lancaster County since 1983. The first time I saw him was at the beginning of one of his camps. He was calling together a bunch of youngsters, his baldness concealed under a baseball cap, and telling them: "I'm the old one. I'm older than a dinosaur."

For years Gabriel and Mario and their soccer buddies participated in his camps. Just before Saúl died, Skip Skip stopped by our house to drop off flyers for the upcoming camp and sat and chatted with Saúl about the strengths and weaknesses of Colombian soccer. Colombia was about to face soccer powerhouse England in a friendly game in New Jersey. "Colombians are going to struggle with the English speed," Skip said. He ignored Saúl's painfully swollen arm and his overall decline, focusing instead their mutual love for soccer. "I know," Saúl said. "It's going to be a tough game."

After Saúl's funeral, so many friends avoided mentioning what had happened, preferring to disregard the subject or treat it only obliquely. "How are you holding up?" was one of the most direct ways my friends acknowledged my loss. But at the soccer camp that was held a month after Saúl died, Skip made me stand up in front of the entire crowd at parents' night. "Becky has suffered a terrible loss. Her wonderful husband died of cancer last month," he said. "But she keeps going and playing soccer. She helped set up the camp and I think we all owe her a round of applause."

Now, eating my crepes, I smiled as I remembered all the good times we have had at Skip's camps. But then I came back to reality.

"Wait a second," I said. "Back home, I *pay* to send you guys to soccer camp. I don't actually put the camp on myself."

"But you can, mom. You know enough soccer and I can help with the activities," Gabriel insisted.

The idea appealed to me. But I wondered how the neighborhood would take to it. The concept of a soccer camp could very well be as foreign to people here as a summer vacation in December was to me. Some of the local families could barely feed and clothe their children, much less worry about signing them up for a vacation soccer camp. But the parents had made one thing clear to me; they did want their kids to learn English.

"Can't you open a little English school right here in the neighborhood?" had been about the second thing my neighbor, Eliana, had said to me when I arrived in August.

After I typed the flyer, Gabriel noticed it was rather bland and he used his growing computer skills to assign each line of text a different color. We argued about whether to try to get the families to pay. I wanted to make the camp free, because I knew some of the parents would not be able to pay, but Gabriel insisted that we include a nominal fee. We argued about it and finally settled on 5,000 pesos, or about $2.50. I knew Gabriel had a point. Saúl had always encouraged me to help people help themselves. Giving too much away doesn't help people, he said, it just encourages them to see themselves as helpless.

Gabriel and Mario were excited about the idea. They printed out the flyers and then taped them to the light posts around the neighborhood. We went to

Bogotá to buy cones, soccer balls, prizes, and the all important coaches' whistle. Gabriel chatted up the camp and the prizes to all his friends in the neighborhood. Then we sat back and waited for the registrations to come flying in.

But they didn't.

Getting sign-ups was going to require the personal touch. Gabriel went three doors down to invite Javier, 14, and Juan Diego, 6. He came back a few minutes later clutching a 10,000 peso note and two signed registration forms.

"Mom, I have good news and bad news. The good news is that both Javier and Juan Diego are signed up and paid in full," he said. "The bad news is that we really need to work hard on the language-school part. Their mother thinks they're going to know English by the end of the week."

"I guess I better come up with an actual curriculum," I said. I sat down at the computer and tried to think of what kind of English I could teach the kids. With the exception of a short stint as a volunteer literacy coach in Brownsville, Texas, I had no experience teaching English. I made up some worksheets that would give them a basis on which to talk, read and write in English. Each one was based on a soccer topic such as "My Soccer Story," or "The Rules of Soccer."

Little by little most of the neighborhood kids signed up. But Christian, eight, and Felipe, 10, two of the most dedicated soccer players in the neighborhood, did not. Their father had died in a car accident a few years earlier and their mother worked hard as a waitress just trying to keep them fed and dressed. Gloria lived two doors down from them, so she knew that the father could have filed for a type of insurance that would have paid off the house if he died, but he had never bothered. Colombia does offer very small stipends to widowed mothers who cannot find work, but there is nothing like the benefits that widows receive in the United States. Because my children were minors, I received about $20,000 a year from Social Security. But the minimum annual wage in Colombia—which Christian and Felipe's mother would probably be lucky to earn—is about $2,400. Understandably, her boys often wore old clothes and sometimes went barefoot.

I invited myself over. Unlike other homes in the neighborhood, there was no living room furniture and the paint on the walls was old and chipped.

"I know 10,000 pesos ($5) for two boys is a lot of money," I said to the mother, María.

I did not mention that soccer camps in the United States cost about 100 times that amount.

"Can you pay for one and the other can go for free?" I asked, and María readily agreed.

Another one of the best soccer players in the neighborhood, Bryan, said he could not afford the 5,000 either. I told his mother she could pay whenever she had the money.

By the Sunday before the camp was supposed to start, we had 18 boys signed up. I nervously made lists of what I planned to teach them and copied out the worksheets for the English classes.

My heart was pounding on the morning of the first day. I brought out the new soccer balls and the cones. Some of the early arrivals grabbed the balls and began running up and down the soccer court, kicking the ball at the goal. What in the world had I gotten myself into? The group ranged from tiny little Santiago, who was five, and his good buddy, also a Santiago, who was six, all the way up to Javier, who was 14 and regularly played soccer with the highly-skilled neighborhood 20-something guys.

"Niños, por favor sientanse!" *Children, come and sit down please.*

There was no response.

"NIÑOS!"

Little by little they settled down on the cement steps that line the soccer court.

I explained that we would have an hour of English every morning and two hours of soccer skills. We would take a lunch break and then have some kind of fun contest before we started the afternoon tournaments. At the end of each day, there would be a prize for the person who behaved the best during the day. "And I'm going to keep throwing in English words during the day," I added.

I passed out the language worksheets and some pencils and began talking about soccer in English.

"Look, here is the English work for today," I said. "My Soccer Story."

The kids looked at me blankly and then started talking among themselves about the worksheet.

"Por favor escúcheme!" *Please listen!*

Most of them paid attention as I went over "My Soccer Story" and explained the parts I wanted them to fill in, such as how long they had been playing soccer and their favorite professional players and teams. I made them all read the worksheet together, out loud. Then I told them that Gabriel, Mario and I would help them individually with the writing in English.

Gabriel sat with five-year-old Santiago and wrote out the whole worksheet for him. Mario answered questions here and there. I reviewed the worksheets and forced myself to speak as much English as possible to each child. After about an hour, everyone had written their own "My Soccer Story" in English.

We read the completed stories together. "I ... have ... played ... soccer ... since ... I ...was (fill in the blank) years old," we read slowly together. "My favorite professional player is ..."

Exhausted after only the first hour, I was relieved when it was finally time to start playing soccer. Somehow I got through the first morning, though the degree of culture clash surprised me. The little kids seemed very inattentive and the older kids told me exactly what was wrong with my skills-building activities. Christian seemed to have a severe case of attention deficit disorder. He likes soccer and he's a good player, but he showed up on Monday morning wearing sandals and he seemed to have left his brain at home.

During one activity, the kids were supposed to pass a ball around a diamond made of cones and follow each pass to the next cone. I explained the activity as clearly and as carefully as I possibly could. But while I was explaining it, Christian was kicking a ball into the goal, so once the activity started, he was completely lost. I worried about him getting hurt from playing soccer in sandals, but he had been doing it for so long that he seemed to be able to use his bare feet just as well as the other kids used their sneakers.

"Pass with your right foot and then jog to the next cone!" I yelled in English. "Quiero decir, patea con el pie derecho!"

During lunch my staff (Gabriel) and I made the teams for the two against two tournament. But for the four against four "World Cup" tournament, we decided the players themselves could pick the teams.

In the afternoon, we started the tournaments, which would last all week. One of the two teen-agers refereed the smaller children's game while I watched over the older players.

Javier, who at 14 was rumored to have been kicked out of two different schools, was determined to win his two against two game. But when the time was up and I blew the whistle to end the game, Javier's team had lost.

"This is not fair! You should have stopped the clock when the ball went out!" he yelled.

I had talked earlier about how all the players must shake hands after each game.

But Javier ignored the rule and stalked off the field. The other kids shrugged; they were used to Javier's lack of sportsmanship. I also decided to let him cool off rather than confront him.

Javier's rival for the week was Julian. While Javier was hot tempered and misbehaved, Julian was calm and polite. They were both highly-skilled soccer players who had known each other since kindergarten. The other two captains were Gabriel and Juan David, who are also good players but not quite at Julian and Javier's level of skill and speed. Fired up after losing in the two-against-two tournament, Javier led his World Cup team, Argentina, to victory in his first World Cup game. With Javier doing most of the work, dribbling madly by the other players and only occasionally passing to his munchkin teammates, Argentina beat Gabriel's Brazil team, 10 to 8.

This time, both sides respected my "fair play" injunction. They formed two lines and shook hands, repeating the American mantra, "Good game, good game, good game."

Most children can mimic pretty well, but English vowels are hard for Spanish speakers.

They tended to pronounce "good" as if it rhymed with "crude." I also tried to teach them to say, "Fair play," the rubric under which the international soccer federation puts all their sportsmanship guidelines.

Finally, at about 3:30 p.m., I reminded everyone to be on time the next day and sent them home. I staggered inside, sat down for a few minutes and then realized I needed to pick up a few things at Don Jorge's store for dinner. Just before I entered the store, Felipe rode up to me on his bike, his eyes shining and a big smile on his face. "The first day was so cool!" he said.

"I'm glad you liked it," I said. "See you tomorrow."

I went back home with a bit more spring in my step. The next few days went fairly smoothly, though there were plenty of moments of exhaustion and frustration.

Often by 11 a.m. the sun was very bright. I wore a wide-brimmed hat and lots of sunscreen. Christian wore sneakers one day and I congratulated him. But the next day he was in back in sandals.

"What happened to your sneakers?" I asked.

"I got yelled at for wearing those sneakers," he told me. "They are only for trips to Bogotá."

Juan Diego, Javier's little brother, dropped out because it turned out that he had school for most of that week. I felt as though I should have refunded his mother's 5,000 pesos, but Javier, the older brother, was such a handful that I decided to keep the money.

On Thursday afternoon, the sky turned a dark gray followed soon after by a huge downpour. The drains on the street below the soccer court got clogged and a river formed where the street had been. "A swimming pool!" one of the kids said as he ran for the water.

"No!" I yelled. "You must never play in floodwaters! They are very dangerous. Everybody go home!"

When I worked at the *Austin American-Statesman*, I wrote many stories about people who died because they drove their cars into floodwaters. Police and firefighters were always asking us to tell our readers to stay away from floodwaters.

"But we want to continue with the tournament!" Javier said. He looked at me with pleading on his big brown eyes. "Tomorrow I might have to go to my brother's graduation."

"What happens, happens, Javier. I can't be responsible for all these kids being out here with these floodwaters," I said. "Everybody go home."

It seemed as though they were leaving, so I went inside. But a few minutes later, I realized that Javier had recruited a referee and he was organizing the games that were scheduled for that day. And here I had thought that my opinions were so important.

I gave up trying to cancel the camp for that day and just sat on the bench and watched as the skies cleared, the floodwaters drained, and the soccer continued.

The next morning we held the finals for all the tournaments. I enjoy almost every aspect of teaching children soccer. The only thing I don't like about coaching soccer is refereeing games. I know I'm not a good referee and I have never taken the courses I need to improve my skills. All week I struggled to make the right call, and to make it quickly.

By the end of the week, some of the unemployed young men in the neighborhood had heard about the tournament and were showing up to watch games. A ball went off the field, and I signaled for Julian's team, Portugal, to restart the play with a throw-in. Apparently this was a bad call because suddenly I heard a deafening yell in my ear.

"AAAYYY Rebecca, if you are going to be the ref, you've got to do a better job!" This from one of the unemployed soccer crazy 20-somethings, Cesar. "Why don't you let me take the whistle?"

I gratefully accepted his offer to referee the final of the World Cup, which was between Javier's team, Argentina, and Julian's team, Portugal. It was an exciting, high-scoring game. Julian's team won, 8 to 7. I watched carefully to see how Javier would handle the defeat, which I knew would be hard for him to take. But it seemed he had learned something.

"Fair play!" a child yelled, rolling the R in "fair" but otherwise pronouncing it well.

Javier approached Julian and shook his hand, and the rest of the players followed suit.

I handed out the medals we had bought in Bogotá, wishing I could give one to Javier. I made everyone pose for a camp picture.

"I had a lot of fun teaching you soccer and English this week," I told the kids. "I hope you keep playing soccer and practicing English. And remember 'Fair Play.'"

The kids smiled and nodded, and ran off to show their parents their awards and their English worksheets, which I had stapled together with a thank you note to the parents. Javier's aunt, whose son, Juan Camilo, was also in the camp, came out of her house with a smile on her face.

"This has been such a blessing," she said. "It's been so good for the kids to be with you all week."

I smiled and thanked her.

"Juan Camilo was a pleasure to teach," I said. "I had a wonderful time with all the kids."

It actually was true.

Ten

A Colombian Christmas

I remember a journey with my uncle Ibañez, a tiger of the Colombian countryside. In those days, we had to leave his house (a straw hut with a zinc roof) and travel to Cachipay with mules loaded with fruit to sell at the market. I remember I studied in the city and easily became so accustomed to the urban life that I would quickly forget how screwed the peasant's life is and it would be difficult to get back into that rhythm. It was the first time I took that three-hour trip on paths that were hard even for the mules. I was in front, leading the train, riding an old gray mule, who was as hard as a rock. Frequently we would come to a fork in the road and I would yell back to my uncle, "which way here?" and he would shout, "to the left, man!" And so like that several times I stopped the whole march because I did not know the way. All the stopping and doubts were slowing down the progress. Finally, my uncle got tired of so many questions and yelled, "let the mule find the way, he knows it better than you do." And it was like that. Imagine, for this old gray mule it was just a matter of loosening the reins and he led all the riders exactly to where the town had to be! Meanwhile I was up there with the fruit and overwhelmed in my mind thinking, "Hell, I don't know shit about the country."

From Saúl Murcia's 2004 letter

" Blessings! I have so many..."

Flor, Saúl's mother, was leading the hymn as we sat in the farmhouse living room on Christmas Eve. "Blessings! God sends me more."

We spent Christmas and New Year's at the farm where Saúl had spent his childhood holidays. And just as Saúl had done as a boy, we gathered in the evening to pray, recite Bible verses and sing hymns.

It was a special time with Saúl's mother, somewhat complicated by our dog, Crystal. In general Crystal adapted very well to life in Colombia. She barked outrageously at anybody who knocked on the door, ate whatever was put in front of her, and was fat and happy. The first time Gloria took her for a walk, Gloria unhooked her leash in a pasture near the barrio and Crystal took off for the horizon. Gloria yelled for her to come back, pronouncing her name the way crystal is pronounced in Spanish: "CREESTAL!" Crystal kept running. Again Gloria yelled "CREESTAL!" And again our dog continued her speedy journey to the edge of the large field. Finally Gloria realized her mistake, contorted her mouth to form the awkward (for her) English vowel, and yelled "Crystal" in the English pronunciation. The moment Crystal heard her named pronounced in the manner to which she was accustomed, she turned tail and came running back to Gloria. Normally, we took turns walking Crystal around the neighborhood, surprising people by always carrying a bag to clean up after her.

Though Crystal had been doing very well in Colombia, she began having hormonal problems in November and by December she had suffered a few incidents of vaginal prolapse. The first time it happened, about an inch of vaginal tissue suddenly appeared hanging from her bottom. I rushed her to Dr. Villarreal. He is the older, more experienced of the two veterinarians in La Mesa. He reinserted the vaginal tissue and told me an exaggerated heat cycle was causing the problem. Dogs, he said, don't go through menopause.

"She urgently needs a complete hysterectomy, but at her age and considering the inflammation of her reproductive organs, it's a high-risk procedure," he said, speaking kindly and calmly. "You should take her to Bogotá for the surgery."

My sons love Crystal, and I enjoy her, but I really did not want to go to the hassle or the expense of taking her to Bogotá for surgery, especially considering dogs were not allowed on the buses. Instead, I took her about a block up the main road in La Mesa to Dr. Jorge.

He examined Crystal quickly and then smiled, his high cheekbones high lighting his bright eyes. He wore his long black hair tied back in a pony tail.

"Give her some antibiotics to prevent infection," he said. "We'll wait about two weeks for the swelling to go down, and then bring her back for the surgery."

"Are you sure?" I said, looking doubtfully around the hectic one-room clinic.

"This will be absolutely no problem," Dr. Jorge answered.

And he was right. On Dec. 28, I brought Crystal back to Dr. Jorge's office. As Dr. Jorge and his wife anesthetized Crystal and performed the surgery, I sat in a nearby chair with Jaime, the owner of the Internet company that had been providing my house with fairly consistent, fairly high-speed Internet service for the past two months. Jaime had been friends with Dr. Jorge ever since the veterinarian saved his dog's life from a potentially fatal poisoning, and he seemed to have a habit of stopping by the office to visit. Jaime was born and raised in California, but twice during his childhood, he lived with his grandparents for a year in order to learn Spanish.

"Those years were always important," Jaime said as we waited for the surgery to end. "I always returned to the United States with more self-confidence, more willingness to see myself as a leader."

I smiled and nodded appreciatively, thinking how surprising it was to meet such an introspective Californian here in small-town Colombia.

A few days after the surgery, I put the recovering Crystal in her crate and brought her to the farm for the New Year's celebration. I was a little embarrassed about the situation, because I knew Grandmother Flor would not like the idea of a dog inside her house, but I did not want to leave her with friends so soon after her surgery. But Flor was just happy to see us.

At 85, Flor was increasingly frail. Her husband had died on June 9, 2006, exactly 365 days after my Saúl died. Flor had lived on the farm for decades, and she did not see being an 85-year-old widow as a good reason for giving up her beloved farmhouse and land. Flor's children were more and more concerned about her determination to stay on the farm alone. They had tried to hire live-in help, but Flor did not like the idea and came up with endless reasons why each person did not suit her. She was also becoming more hard of hearing.

Over the holidays, I had an odd desire to just sit and be with her, even if conversation was difficult. Instead of helping out with the numerous chores that always needed to be done on the farm, I often sat next to her as she ate or read the Bible. She had been coughing lately and the rhythm of her breathing seemed agitated.

She nonetheless participated in the holiday celebrations and eagerly led us in prayer and hymn singing in the evening.

On New Year's Eve, about eight of the barrio's teen-agers and twenty-somethings brought brooms and started sweeping the long narrow street that winds through the neighborhood. They started in the morning and swept and swept all day. At the end of the day, with the street clean and ready for the New Year, they went door to door asking for contributions, which I suspect were spent on booze for that night's celebration.

On New Year's Day we went back to the farm and I took the children to river, which was flowing a little stronger than usual because of recent rains. Gabriel sat in the white water between two rocks and then dared to put his head back into the pounding current. "It's like a Jacuzzi, Mom! You have to try it." I braved the cold water and dipped my head back too. The water swirled over me at high speed for as long as I could use my arms and legs to resist the pull. Finally I climbed out from between the two rocks, a little shaky from the exertion but very exhilarated. "I feel like a million bucks," I told Gabriel as he paddled by on a toy inflatable boat.

We played like that until the sun began to set behind the tall bamboo trees that bordered the river. We trekked back up the hill, passing the rock where Saúl used to hide from the stress of his large family and all the farm work. We walked by the site of the bamboo house Saúl's father built when they first moved to the land when Saúl was a young boy. Now the area is filled with banana plants.

As I peered through the thick vegetation at the spot where I first tasted Flor's potato soup, I thought of the plaque the site merited: "Here two brave pioneers, Flor and Saúl Murcia, built their original bamboo house, and worked the land from before dawn to after dusk to raise seven children. Although they had little of their own, they were strong believers in the gospel and always shared whatever they could with their neighbors."

We arrived at the farm house, and found that everyone was wondering about us. "Finally!" Flor said from her seat by the window. "We were getting ready to send somebody to look for you," said her daughter, Flor.

The next day the sisters decided that grandmother Flor should go to La Mesa so a doctor could check her cough. We grabbed our bags and walked slowly up the rock track that leads to the dirt road that goes by the farm. As Flor trudged up the hill with a cane, I looked around at the huge palm trees and the orange and coffee plants. Gloria and Flor were walking with us. "This reminds me of the last time I walked my father away from the farm," Gloria said, remembering that her father had died a year and a half earlier. "But this is different. Our mom will be back at the farm soon," her sister answered.

After the doctor's visit, the sisters brought their mother to Gloria's house so they could monitor her health more closely. The doctor thought she had bronchitis and prescribed antibiotics and cough medicine. Over the next few days, she seemed to improve, though she still seemed weak and a little listless.

On Monday morning, Cesar and his girlfriend, Naomi, asked me if I would play with them in a three on three volleyball tournament that was being held because the holidays had brought so many visitors to the neighborhood. Naomi is very athletic and Cesar can cover a lot of ground and hit the ball hard. We had played pick up volleyball several times before so our teamwork was fairly good. We were bumping, setting and hitting well and for much of the day we were unbeatable. I was caught up in the excitement of the tournament while Gabriel and Mario played with their friends. During a lunch break, I remembered I should check on Flor at Gloria's. I brought Gabriel and Mario with me so they could visit with her a little. She was sitting upstairs, watching Animal Planet on the television. I greeted her quickly. As I was hurrying away to get back to the tournament, Flor startled me with a question. There was a tone of urgency in her voice. "Did you go to church yesterday?" she asked. Mario had been ill with allergies during the night and slept until 11 a.m., so we had not gone to church.

"No," I answered lamely. "Mario was not well."

"Oh," she said, not voicing her disappointment. I continued down the stairs. When the volleyball tournament ended, my sons and I went directly home, ate dinner, read together and went to sleep. The next morning Saúl's brother, Edilberto, knocked on my door early.

"I'm here to take my mother back to the clinic. But first we need help getting her dressed," he told me. Alarm bells went off in my head. "She needs help getting dressed?" I asked, unable to believe that the feisty woman who had interrogated me about church attendance the night before now needed help dressing herself. I walked quickly to Gloria's house and went upstairs. Yuri, the youngest daughter, was kneeling on Gloria's double bed, holding her mother's upper body in her arms.

"Becky! What should we do?" Yuri asked me, her voice full of fear. Flor's eyes were closed and her head was tilted back. Her limbs had the flaccid droop of an unconscious person. "She just greeted me so cheerfully. I don't know what happened."

Edilberto and Gloria took one look and said they were going to get an ambulance. I rushed to the bedside, frantically trying to think of what to do.

"I think we should lay her down flat," I said.

Yuri gently set her mother's upper body down on the bed. She was no longer breathing. I looked around for Gloria and Edilberto, but only Yuri was there.

"Do you want me to do CPR?"

"Yes, please," said Yuri in a whisper.

I took a deep breath, tilted Flor's head back, and pinched her nose. Her dentures immediately fell off into her mouth. I grabbed the teeth and set them on the bedside table. I took another deep breath and blew. But it was as though there was no place for the air to go.

I stood up and pressed both hands to her chest, trying to remember the last first aid class I had taken 12 years earlier. I pressed her chest rhythmically 15 times, and then tried the breathing routine again. I did another 15 chest compressions.

"I think she's gone," Yuri said.

I felt her wrist for a pulse, but all I could feel was the blood flowing rapidly through my own fingers.

"Should I stop?" I asked Yuri.

"Yes," she said, bursting into tears. "I think we need to let her go."

I cried, too. I felt Grandma Flor's hand growing colder. I arranged the blanket neatly over her lower body. Yuri began calling all the sisters.

"I'll go call Eligia," I said and walked unsteadily back to my house.

"Flor died," I said to the boys as I walked in the door. "I need to call Eligia."

I entered Eligia's office number at the National Institutes of Health in Bethesda, Maryland, into my laptop phone calling program. "Good morning, Eligia speaking," I heard Eligia's cheerful, professional greeting on her office phone. I burst into tears again.

"What's happening? I can't hear you!" I heard Eligia saying.

I gathered my strength to say the words I knew Eligia would hate to hear.

"I'm so sorry, Eligia," I said. "Your mom died."

"No! I can't believe it!" Eligia said, the shock coming across the Internet and booming into my little living room.

I told her what had happened and promised to talk to her again soon.

By then Gabriel was awake and both boys were downstairs sitting on the couch. I gave them hugs and told them I was sorry their grandmother was dead.

"How did it happen so fast?" Gabriel said, frowning. "She wasn't that sick yesterday..."

"Pneumonia is like that," I said. "Sometimes people die very quickly."

Gabriel and Mario nodded their heads.

"Boys," I said, "There are going to be a lot of people here over the next few days and I want us to try to be good hosts."

Again they nodded their heads. I arrived back at Gloria's house just as the paramedic was arriving to take Flor to the hospital. He held a stethoscope to Flor's still chest.

"Her lungs are completely filled with fluid," he said before leaving.

Gloria and Edilberto came back, took one look, and left again to begin making arrangements.

We were sitting in Gloria's living room, drinking coffee and recovering from our shock, when a cousin I did not know appeared. The cousin was accompanied by his wife and small child. He was dressed in a nice cotton shirt and name brand Lee jeans. Over the years I had heard references to a cousin who was involved in drug trafficking and I wondered if this stranger was the one. I looked at Saúl's brother's and sisters' faces for clues. But everybody was either too distracted or too polite to pull me aside.

"I'd like to meet your sons," the cousin said, while his son nodded eagerly.

I invited them to my house, half afraid and half trusting that somebody would have found some way to let me know if this cousin was *that* cousin. I served the coffee and Gabriel and Mario played computer games with their son.

"It's so good to finally meet you," he said. "Here, take down my cell phone number in case you ever need anything."

Obediently I added his cell phone number to my address book and my cell phone directory.

Soon Gloria came over, at which time the family left, promising to return for Flor's funeral. Gloria took a cup of coffee and sat down on the couch. I asked her about the mysterious cousin.

"You didn't take down his number, did you?"

"Yes, I have it right here in my cell phone," I answered.

"What! You put his cell phone number in your cell phone? You must delete it right away," Gloria said. "He's been in jail for drug trafficking three times."

I turned over these new events in my mind—the shock of Flor's death, the sudden appearance of the mysterious cousin. I wanted to believe that maybe he had changed.

"What does he claim to do for a living?" I asked Gloria.

"He *claims* that he buys and sells produce—which is true in a way," she said with a little laugh.

Saúl had never really spoken directly to me of his uncle Ibañez's children. But I remembered a moment many years earlier when he mentioned them in passing. Mennonites don't believe in baptizing infants. But they do hold a blessing ceremony in which the parents promise to raise their children well. Gabriel was a few months old when we held his blessing ceremony in Austin, Texas. Saúl, who never liked to disclose personal details in public, stood up and moved everyone by recalling his childhood in the mountains of Colombia.

"My mother's brother was poor just like we were. The only real difference was that my mother was a Christian and tried to raise us within the church," he said. "Her brother was not a Christian. Her brother's children, my cousins, have been in a lot of trouble, including going to prison for drug trafficking."

On that occasion, Saúl's eyes disclosed—however briefly—the pain he felt over the situation with his cousin. He never mentioned that branch of the family again. But a year or so later I saw a letter asking if Saúl could visit a cousin who was in federal prison in Texas. I don't think we even talked about it; but I remember thinking that this cousin would have to manage without a visit from Saúl because Saúl had made it clear he wanted nothing to do with these cousins.

This was exactly the type of thing that would have made Saúl nervous about us going to Colombia without him. The black sheep in the family, the ones who could potentially get me in a lot of trouble, could appear without warning.

I decided to try not to think about the cousin too much. There were plenty of other things to worry about. The next day, I went to the funeral home and sat with the young man who had been Flor's pastor during the last few years of her life. We sang, "Blessings! I have so many!" It made me cry, singing Flor's favorite hymn as she lay there in her coffin, gone forever.

That evening Gabriel and Mario helped me make carmelitas (caramel oatmeal bars) and coffee brownies. I didn't know if there was going to be a reception or not, but I wanted to be ready. We ended up serving some of them for breakfast the next morning, when Armando, one of Saúl's nephews who lives in Canada, arrived with his wife and children.

The Mennonite Church of La Mesa was packed with Flor's many friends and relatives. Speaker after speaker remembered her courage and faith. Little Juliana, Edilberto's daughter, drew the most laughs when she told the crowd. "I learned many things from my grandmother, including how to eat onions."

After the service, pallbearers loaded the coffin into an old station wagon and we all followed on foot, singing hymns, until we arrived at the cemetery and slid the box into one of the spaces on the huge walls, which are deep enough to hold rows upon rows of coffins. The cemetery was rather forbidding, with the words "remove remains" written on several of the spaces where coffins were stored. I learned later "remove remains" are notes intended for the families of the deceased who have not kept up with the cemetery maintenance fees. What I do not know is whether the church authorities follow through with the threat.

We made our way home and found that Pedro Stucky, the older brother of Saúl's dear childhood friend, Tim Stucky, and his family had arrived just as the funeral was ending. We gathered in Gloria's house, grateful to continue remembering Flor and her amazing life. A few brownies remained.

Eleven

CARTAGENA

The 10-day trip to the coast was like a giant yes that life had given me. There were so many things that I lived, felt, understood, heard and suddenly many empty spaces about what it meant to be a Colombian were filled. It was a huge, unexpected affirmation after long years of negatives, embarrassment, struggles with anxiety and poverty in cycles since my infancy. It was something like a huge prize to graduate from high school—sort of an honorific representation of my parents' generation, who scarcely learned to read and write because their lives were so difficult.

From Saúl Murcia's 2004 letter about his high school graduation trip to the coast in 1976

Colombian airports are extremely security conscious. People who are waiting for loved ones are not allowed inside. So Gabriel, Mario and I were part of a crowd that was waiting behind a metal fence outside the Cartagena airport while my mother and her best friend, Judith, went through immigration and customs. I left home when I was 17 years old and went for months without calling my parents when I was in college. I was not estranged, just busy. But when I became a mother I became close to my mother again. And when Saúl was incapacitated by cancer, my mother came with all her homespun wisdom and her occupational therapy skills and helped us with everything from wheelchair mechanics to washing, drying and folding clothes.

When she volunteered to come and visit us in Colombia, along with Judith, I was thrilled. We decided to meet in Cartagena, a tourist-friendly Colombian city on the Caribbean. Cartagena is famous for its beautiful beaches and its old walled city, which took 200 years to build. "I will be there on Jan. 19," my mother wrote to me in an e-mail. "Book us a nice hotel. Start with the Hilton and work down from there."

When Saúl and I had gone to Cartagena in 1992 we had visited a travel agent in Bogotá that sold us an "all-included" vacation. We were to be joined by Saúl's boyhood friend, Timothy and Timothy's wife, Luzdy. Timothy's parents had founded the boarding school for the children of lepers that Saúl and his siblings had attended. He and Saúl became best friends when they were in first grade. Three decades later Timothy and Luzdy were serving as community development volunteers for the Mennonite Central Committee at the same campus, which had since been turned into a retreat center. Timothy was trying to promote peace in the area surrounding the former school. It was a difficult task.

The main guerilla army that had been fighting the government for decades, the Revolutionary Armed Forces of Colombia, signed a peace agreement in 1985. The pact called for the guerillas to lay down their arms and form a legal political party. The guerillas created the Patriotic Union and began nominating candidates for office. But death squads systematically exterminated the party members and the candidates. The party continued, somehow, for about 10 years. Jaime Pardo Leal, a former presidential candidate, was assassinated in 1987 near La Mesa. Another candidate for the presidency, Bernardo Jaramillo, was assassinated in 1990.

The lesson for the peasants? The government or forces allied with the government will meet peaceful movements for political change with violence. The peasants of Cachipay had learned the lesson well, and they were not particularly open to Timothy's teaching. At one dinner, Timothy talked about how all the neighbors were furious because a rich landowner in the area was polluting the river that everyone used for drinking water. He called a meeting and tried to explain about non-violent conflict resolution—a Mennonite specialty. But one of the farmers said, "'Let's just send the guerillas in,' and I had to push hard to prevent everybody from agreeing that calling the guerillas was the best solution," Timothy recalled.

Saúl was eager to give his friends an enjoyable vacation. At the same time, he was concerned that the whole "all-included" concept was too good to be true. The travel agency had promised us tours, meals and a hotel room for the price, which had included the air fare. On the flight to Cartagena, Saúl joked nervously about how the Comodore hotel where we supposedly had reservations probably did not really exist. "Our hotel is probably going to be the Sea Breeze Hotel," he said. To confirm Saúl's suspicions, when we arrived, the taxi driver said he had not heard of the Comodore. "I said it was not for real," Saúl said. But then the taxi driver checked with a friend and found out that indeed, a hotel called the Comodore did exist. He took us to the hotel, which was brand new, and we had a great time with his Colombian friends, touring the city and enjoying good conversation and fine meals. And everything really was included.

One of the reasons my mother and I had decided to meet in Cartagena was that mosquitoes find my mother particularly delicious, *and* she is allergic to their bites. I was afraid she would be eaten alive in La Mesa. I did not remember seeing any mosquitoes during our 1992 trip. But a few days before my mom's flight, she was reading about Cartagena on the Internet and came across the line: "Mosquitoes are ubiquitous in Cartagena." She e-mailed me in a panic: "What have you gotten me into?"

I told her I was pretty sure the website she was reading was wrong, but that she should pack plenty of repellent just in case. As the date approached, I was excited, but I was also feeling a little nervous. How was I going to manage the vacation needs and wants of two boys and two seventy-something grandmothers?

But I forged ahead with the plans and was looking forward to the upcoming visit. After taking an earlier flight from Bogotá to Cartagena, Gabriel, Mario and I waited with the crowd outside the airport. The wait seemed interminable, as we tried to peer through the tinted windows to see if our guests were arriving. I thought I caught a glimpse of my mother, but the sun was so bright it was hard to see through the tinted glass. Passengers began slowly making their way through the door, past the metal gate, and out to where their friends and relatives were waiting for them. My mother appeared at the door. I couldn't help myself. I dashed through the security gate and grabbed my mother in a fierce hug. "I can't believe you came all this way!" I said. "I am so happy." The security agents remained calm. Apparently they were used to emotion getting the better of people. My children, however, took a while to forgive me. "Mom," Gabriel said, after he had given my mother a calmer, less emotional hug and we were all loaded up in two taxis. "That was *so* embarrassing."

"We made it!" Judith said with a big smile. Judith and my mom have been friends since the 1960s, when they marched against the Vietnam War together.

Our two taxis pulled up at the Hotel Estelar Almirante. I had tried the Hilton, but it was full. The Almirante, with its eleven-story towers and its glass exterior walls was a bit modern for our tastes, but it had received great reviews on the Internet. Porters met our taxis and loaded our luggage onto their carts. We walked into the hotel's large lobby, with its tropical plants and its gleaming floor. "This is beautiful," my mom said, looking around.

My mom and Judith checked in and we all went to their room for the ritual opening of the suitcases. "Here my dear," said my mother, as she handed me Patrick Symme's new book about Fidel Castro and Cuba, *Hijos de Dolores*, and *More*, the magazine for middle-aged women. She had presents for Gabriel and Mario, plus the underwater cameras I had suggested for our snorkeling adventure.

The next morning a smartly uniformed waiter, wearing the iconic black and white straw hat of the Colombian coast, showed us to our seats at the hotel's elegant breakfast buffet. Another waiter approached with a pot of hot milk in one hand and a pot of hot coffee in the other. He carefully poured my coffee and then added the milk until it was just the lightness I like. I tasted it and then rose to help myself to a plateful of fruit, yogurt and pastry at the buffet. Returning to the table, I announced, "This is the life."

After breakfast, we shopped and wandered around for a while, we ventured out on to the public beach in front of the hotel.

"ZAPATOS (shoes)!" a street seller yelled as he brandished water shoes under our noses

"FRUTA!" yelled another as she walked by carrying a tray full of mangos and coconuts.

"MASSAGES!" yelled a young woman. "BRAIDS!"

The vendors were a little overwhelming, but we quickly learned that a quick shake of the head and a look away was better than a polite, "no thank you." The vendors would take a polite "no thank you" as an opening of negotiations. We left Judith sunning herself on the beach and hurried to the water. We plunged into the choppy waves, delighted to let the water wash over us. After we had been swimming for a little while, two young men with boogie boards came up to us. At first I thought, *oh, no the vendors won't even leave us alone out there in the water*. But they made an offer we couldn't refuse. They said they would teach Gabriel and Mario to surf the waves on the boogie boards for half an hour for the equivalent of $5 each. The boys were eager to ride the boogie boards, so my mother and I agreed and continued swimming as they raced back and forth in the waves. Both the young men seemed to be having a good time, too. Mario and Gabriel would each get on a board, and the men would hold the board until a good wave came. At just the right moment, they would each push as hard as they could, and Gabriel and Mario would race each other to the beach on the wave. Soon Judith joined us in the water and we all enjoyed the waves and the setting sun. "This is just fantastic," Judith said as we walked back to the hotel. "We should do this every afternoon." My unease about the possibility of a vacation that three generations could enjoy together ebbed. I started to relax a little.

We went to the San Felipe castle, a huge fort the Spanish crown had built in Cartagena to protect the city from pirates and marauders who were trying to steal the gold the Spaniards were stealing from Colombia. "I speak English. I am your guide." When Rafael said these words and smiled at us we could not say no, even though his English was shaky at best. Rafael took us all over the castle, through tunnels and around gun turrets. He explained how it fit into the military strategy and where the soldiers hid the arms. Gabriel and Mario pretended to fire a canon as my mother—a passionate photographer—fired off shots with her camera.

That night we had an incredible dinner at a restaurant in the old city. We ordered red snapper and the waiter brought the raw fish out to us on a tray for our inspection. A few minutes later he reappeared with fried fish accompanied by coconut rice and huge plantains that had been smashed and fried so they were sort of like plantain pancakes. "Red snapper is my favorite food in the world," Gabriel declared after picking the last bit of fried fish off the bones.

After another day of touring the city and enjoying the restaurants, we decided we were ready for the Rosary Islands, one of Colombia's two most popular national parks. The bell boys at the hotel set up the trip, and all we had to do was appear at the front door at 8 a.m. We were driven to the docks and then packed into a large motor boat. A row of Chilean twenty-somethings sat behind us and an Argentinean couple sat in front of us. We arrived at an island with a beautiful white beach, a salt water swimming pool, and a few artisans selling handmade jewelry. About half the group was going snorkeling and the other half were going to an aquarium. Once the snorkelers were in the boat, the guides started handing out masks and fins. The boat stopped about a quarter-mile from the shore and everybody started putting on the equipment.

I had no idea the snorkeling would be so far away from the beach. I panicked. *How could I be a lifeguard for my two sons and two septuagenarians in such deep water?* I saw Gabriel, who had already jumped in the water, handing the life jacket to a guide who was still on the boat. "Wait!" I yelled at Gabriel. "Put that life jacket back on!" The guide looked at me as though I had lost my mind. "Mom, I can't snorkel in a life jacket," Gabriel said to me calmly as he finished sending his life jacket back into the boat. I looked around, and I realized my mother and Judith were happily swimming with the guide, and that Mario was holding on to the lifeguard's rescue tube. Soon, we were all paddling away from the boat. The water was warm and perhaps especially salty; I felt very buoyant. The guide pointed out different types of coral and then dove down about 15 feet to retrieve a sea cucumber. He held up the little animal, which really did look like a brown cucumber with warts. He then proudly described its anatomy to us in his best English. "Dis ees dee head," he said, pointing at one end. Then he turned it around and said. "Dis ees dee ass."

The Argentinean couple was supposed to be with us, but the woman, whose name was Luz Marina, or Marine Light, paddled out toward the open sea as though she was on some kind of mission. The guide was troubled by how far away she had gone, so he started yelling, "LUZ MARINA!" But Luz Marina kept swimming off toward the horizon. Every time the guide yelled "LUZ MARINA" Gabriel looked around for this special marine light the guide was seeing. After about five "LUZ MARINA!" shouts, Gabriel finally decided that the guide just thought Marine Light was a wonderful thing, and he stopped trying to find the exact marine light the guide was talking about.

We snorkeled for about an hour, floating easily in the salty water and loving the brightly colored fish and wide variety of corals. Judith and my mother, despite being in their 70s, swam easily and never needed help from me or the guide. Finally Luz Marina rejoined our group and we swam back to the boat. Over a delicious lunch of fried fish back at the island, I told Luz Marina how confused Gabriel had been when the guide kept calling her name. "That's the best story I've ever heard about my name," she said.

For the first few nights at the hotel, we noticed a singer in the bar area strumming a guitar and pouring out his heart in romantic ballads. But we did not stop to listen until the fourth night. There was a ping pong table in a room next to the bar, so we sat down on some lounge chairs near the ping pong table and listened. "Is there anything you would like to hear?" he asked. I immediately thought of Saúl's favorite music.

Saúl had been a fan of vallenato, a form of fast-paced, accordion-based Colombian dance music. His strictly Christian parents frowned on such frivolities, but he had a neighbor, Nelson, who had a radio and the pair would sneak off to hidden spots on the farm to sit and listen to vallenato music on the radio. During a melancholic time after his first cancer surgery, Saúl wrote a letter about music and poetry to his siblings and cousins. "Without knowing it, Nelson gave me the means to survive my exile from Colombia, now for half a life with a hint of disaster. Vallenato music has helped me withstand the discomfort of the distances. Well, what more authentic form of remembering your native land is there than listening to vallenato?" he wrote.

I thought of one of Saúl's favorite vallenatos, one that a band in Austin used to play at a Mexican restaurant we liked. I spoke up. "I can't remember the name, but do you know that Colombian song about the taxi with a certain number that takes away the young love?"

"The vallenato?" the singer answered. "*Zero Treinta y Nueve?*" (Zero-thirty-nine.)

He launched into the song's lively tune and I sat and listened, entranced. I didn't even notice how interested Gabriel and Mario were. We went back the next night and introduced ourselves. The singer, John Jairo Rojo, played Zero Treinta y Nueve for us again and some other favorites. We bought copies of his CD and he signed them with typical Colombian flare. "For Rebecca, Gabriel and Mario with a heartfelt hug."

The next day, as we were winding up our visit, I filled out a survey about our stay at the hotel. I read a question out loud. "Was there anyone at the hotel who particularly helped make your stay wonderful?"

"Put down the guitar dude for that," Gabriel answered quickly. I did.

But it really hit me how much the guitar dude meant a few weeks later, after Gabriel bought "Zero Treinta y Nueve" on iTunes. We began listening to that song and other albums of vallenato music.

Later, after we'd returned to our house in La Mesa, Mario had to write a few lines for Spanish class about somebody he admired. He decided to write about Saúl. I wondered what he was going to say, since Mario was six when Saúl got cancer and eight when he died. "I admire my father, Saúl, because he was always happy," Mario wrote. "He liked the same kind of music I like."

Twelve

BACK TO SCHOOL

Father Jaime Zuleta, one of our teachers, gathered us together in the middle of the street.
The little friar was quite a guy, very full of fun, hard-driving, a good teacher who helped
me a lot with my confused evangelical faith and probably helped me understand the novel
concept that Catholics could also go to heaven! He was one of those stubborn people
who was convinced that it was possible to create a better Colombia, that the young, poor
and humble of Colombia had the talent to move the structures of oppression and exclu-
sion that had us screwed from the time we were in our mothers' wombs. Father Jaime
believed so firmly in us that he was willing to give up his own life for us or at least that
is the type of trust and respect that he inspired in us. He demanded of us academically,
he developed our power of critical thinking; he taught us not to take things at their face
value, but always ask why about everything at a social, political and religious level. And
to boot, he was a diehard lover of our own religion: soccer!
From Saúl's 2004 letter

abriel had arrived in Colombia in August with fairly good Spanish
skills. It was just a matter of a few weeks before he sounded pretty
much like a native speaker. Mario, meanwhile, struggled to become fluent for
the first few months that we lived in Colombia.

By January, they were both fluent speakers with fairly good accents. Gabriel, however, had noticed a deficiency in his Spanish that had completely escaped me. Ever since I was a little girl I've been able to roll my Rs. Maybe my mother taught me or maybe it was my sister, who used to pass along to me some of her high school Spanish. Though I hadn't even noticed that Gabriel could not roll his Rs, the longer he stayed in a school in Colombia, the more attuned his ear became to accents and imperfections in people's Spanish.

One morning he woke up looking extremely worried.

"I dreamed the American officials don't allow people back into the United States unless they can roll their Rs," he said. He gave a little laugh. He knew the dream could not be true, but it underscored how much his inability to roll his Rs was bothering him.

"Try saying butter, butter, butter," I told him. "A friend in college learned to roll her Rs that way."

"Rrrrrrrrr," he said, grimacing as he tried to force his mouth to form the rolling R sound. A guttural growling R came out.

For the next few days he continued to be obsessed. Mario noticed how frustrated Gabriel was and began to demonstrate his own facility by rolling *his* Rs. We were eating chicken soup one night when Mario realized how easy it would be to taunt Gabriel over his obsession. "It's easy," he said. "Just practice. Ferrrrrocarrrril," Mario enunciated, drawing out the way he rolled his Rs perfectly.

Gabriel's face showed how hurt and offended he was. Mario went for the kill.

"I'll say it again. Ferrrrrocarrrril," he pronounced perfectly. (Ferrocarril means railway)

I realized by the pain on Gabriel's face that Mario had gone too far.

"Mario," I said. "Stop. And tell him you're sorry."

"I'm sorrrrry," Mario said, again drawing out the R in "sorry" with perfect rolling pronunciation. Though Gabriel was the butt of the joke he appreciated it anyway, and looked a little less distressed.

"Mario!" As I scolded Mario I had to laugh.

A few days later, Gabriel's obsession bore fruit.

"Mom, listen," he said. "Ferrrrocarrrril," rolling his Rs perfectly.

106

I gave him a hug. "I guess now you can come back with us."

⟶

*G*abriel and Mario went back to school in early February finally leaving me time to wage war against Telecom, the telephone company in Colombia that seemed to be run by the devil himself. When I had first arrived in Colombia, I had signed up for "Unlimited Telephone Internet." There had been a big poster advertising the program at the phone company office, which said that for only 40,000 pesos, or about $20, I could use the Internet as much as I wanted. Being a gullible American I had signed up, obtained a user name and a password, and began using the Internet as much as I wanted. A few months later, I found out that I actually never had been enrolled in "Unlimited Internet," but rather a super expensive by-the-minute Internet plan, and I owed the telephone company something like $500. I tried to pay the bill and cancel the request, because by then I had signed up with a broadband Internet service provider. But the customer service people at Telecom never seemed able to help.

"For the fifth time, can you cancel my telephone Internet service and take that charge off my bill?" I yelled into the telephone one afternoon as thousands of other unhelpful customer service agents chattered in the background.

"Oh, of course, just pay it this one last time and then it will definitely be removed," the operator said.

"But that's what you said when I paid the bill in December and January," I said, sighing in frustration.

In the midst of my tirade, there was a knock on the door and Crystal, as usual, started barking her head off. Mario was home from school.

"Thank you very much," I said into the telephone, not meaning it at all. "Adiós."

"Hola Mario!" I said opening the door. "How was school? I've got a ripe mango here for your snack." I went into the kitchen, washed a mango, and sliced off a big circular chunk off the side. Then I flipped the chunk over and used a sharp little knife to cut the flesh into small squares, and turned the skin inside out so the little cubes I had cut turned into small towers that poked out like the back of a porcupine, or *puercoespin*, as Saúl used to say.

"Mom, I need to read an international news story and write about it," Mario said, sitting down and picking up his mango porcupine to take a bite. He had just started fifth grade at the Liceo Campestre. When we first arrived, Mario was a newcomer in fourth grade who did not know very much Spanish. The teachers had cut Mario lots of slack. But now he had been in Colombia for six months and the teachers had started cracking their whips. "I'd like to find a story in English, with a good picture to go with it," he continued. "I need to memorize my summary and present it in Social Studies tomorrow."

Mario's social studies teacher, who was known as "El Profe Francisco," had been one of the teachers who had been especially nice to Mario and me when we first arrived in La Mesa. Francisco had dark, bushy eyebrows and skin the color of coffee with just a little milk. He always wore jeans belted under his slight paunch and a button-down shirt. For most of the fall, Francisco had ridden Victor Hugo's little white school bus with Mario every morning. He was in charge of opening and closing the sliding door and always had a smile and a greeting for me while Mario climbed into the bus. When Mario started school in the fall, Francisco had given him plenty of time to do a basic geography project. He had written his cell phone number in Mario's notebook in case I had any questions about the maps of La Mesa, the state of Cundinamarca, Colombia, and the Americas that Mario was supposed to trace and color.

When Mario brought up this new assignment, I groaned inwardly. Memorization is one of Mario's weaknesses. "Okay, Sweetie," I said. "Let's start looking." I skimmed through some magazines that were haphazardly piled on top of Crystal's carrying case, which doubled as an end table in our house.

I started leafing through a spectacular edition of *Semana,* which was the Colombian equivalent of *Time* or *Newsweek*. The magazine had sent reporters and photographers to all the remote corners of Colombia and had published a special issue called: "Unknown Colombia."

"We might find something here," I said, scanning the pictures of a Colombian herder escorting goats over a parched landscape and a Colombian cowboy wearing a blue soccer jersey.

"It's supposed to be international, Mom," Mario reminded me of the instructions.

I picked up a *National Geographic* and was looking at a story about New Orleans in the aftermath of Hurricane Katrina.

"This looks interesting," I said. "It's got a lot of information about the hurricane."

"Like I said, Mom. *International*," Mario said.

"Good point, Mario, but since New Orleans is in the United States, it's international in Colombia."

Mario brightened as I explained that New Orleans was, in fact, international. We read the story together and learned about how New Orleans is below sea level and getting lower every year. I went to the laptop and asked Mario what he wanted to say about the story. I gave him suggestions. "How do you say sinking in Spanish?" Mario asked. "Let's see, I think to sink is *hundir,*" I answered after consulting the English-Spanish dictionary I had saved on my hard drive. After about a half hour, we had composed a paragraph about New Orleans. Microsoft Word had added what I thought were most of the proper Spanish accents and tildes, those squiggly lines that sometimes go over the N in Spanish. I printed it out and Mario carefully copied it into his Social Studies notebook. Then he pasted the maps and pictures he had cut out of the *National Geographic*.

While we were doing this Gabriel arrived late from school after dance practice.

"Are you doing Mario's homework for him *again*?" Gabriel said, peering at the computer screen where I had typed our summary of the *National Geographic* article.

"I'm not doing it for him," I said, even though I had been caught somewhat red-handed. "I'm just helping him. It's still hard for Mario to write in Spanish."

Gabriel grimaced. "I wonder why."

By then the usual neighborhood soccer game had started and kids were calling Mario through our open window. Mario headed for the door as I reminded him that he needed to be inside for dinner by 7:30 p.m.

Gabriel, meanwhile, sashayed across the floor, humming a vallenato tune. A dance teacher had chosen Gabriel and seven other boys to prepare a synchronized dance and perform it on International Women's Day on March 8. I glanced at him in amazement as he displayed the salsa-type steps that I had never mastered, despite being married to a Colombian for 16 years. When we first married, I realized that Saúl was an excellent dancer and I often asked him to teach me. "The problem is that I can only dance when I'm drunk and since I'm a Mennonite that almost never happens," he said. Gabriel stopped his rhythmic hip motion as soon as he realized I was watching him. "I'm starting to understand the dance steps we're doing pretty well," he said. "Today I was throwing in my own little moves."

"Can I see?" I asked.

"Oh no," Gabriel said, shaking his head at the thought of demonstrating dance steps to his mother. "You can't see and you can't come to watch on the big day. It would be way too embarrassing."

The next morning Mario and I were sitting in the sunshine at his bus stop, waiting for Victor Hugo to show up with his white school bus. "I need to practice," Mario said, pulling out his notebook. "Este articulo explica que New Orleans está en peligro," Mario read slowly but accurately. "It was fun working on that with you," I said. "I hope the teacher likes it."

I had no idea how much tougher things were going to get. Take biology, for instance. I don't remember even hearing the word cellular when I was in elementary school. My vague memory of high school biology did not include any in-depth study of different types of cells. But a few days after the Social Studies assignment, Mario came home with cellular biology homework that threw me for a loop.

"Define a prokaryotic and a eukaryotic cell."

These teachers have got to be kidding, I thought to myself. I did have vague memories of learning about the nucleus and the membrane of the cell, but I had no memory of these terms. Luckily the Internet was working that day. We read the definitions in Spanish and then we read them in English. "The genetic material in the prokaryotic cell is not membrane-bound," I read at the

Wikipedia website. "Wow, Mario, isn't this interesting? To think I've lived my whole life without knowing that."

We muddled through and came up with one-sentence definitions for the two words. I was already becoming weary of doing homework. "Let's see, now I need to think of three ways to save the environment," Mario continued.

"Well, what did you learn in class about how to protect the environment?" I asked.

"In class we only came up with one: Not Littering," Mario said. "So the teacher told us to think and come up with some more."

At that point I was too tired to be a good teacher. I thought for a moment and said, "Mario, let's just put down: maintain the car well so it doesn't pollute, and don't dump untreated sewage into the rivers."

"I need one more," Mario said.

I thought about something I had really liked about living in Colombia. We rode the green buses back and forth all the time. "Put down walk or ride the bus," I said.

"But Mom, the bus has a big engine," Mario said. "I think it pollutes."

"Yes, it does pollute, but it's going to make the round anyway, so you don't add to the pollution by riding on it," I said.

"I get it," Mario answered as he copied our three ways to save the world into his notebook.

Mario kept coming home from El Liceo Campestre with projects and assignments that were complicated and time consuming. While Francisco continued to be one of Mario's favorite teachers, the homework projects he assigned sometimes astounded me. Mario and I researched and wrote an essay about the Native Americans of the United States, and the advantages and disadvantages of the U.S. election system.

Ironically, Gabriel, who was in the seventh grade at the American Mennonite School, which had a reputation for being the best college preparatory school in La Mesa, did not have anywhere near as much homework. He occasionally worked on a book report, or had to research some terms on the Internet for biology class. But he was often free in the afternoons to play outside or read books while Mario and I slaved away on projects. Even though doing all the projects with Mario was time consuming and sometimes a little mind boggling, I knew it was good practice for Mario. He benefited from all the reading and writing and his ability to read in Spanish kept improving. It was sometimes frustrating, however, that Gabriel had it so much easier, even though he was two grades above Mario.

One day, as I walked to the bus stop with my groceries, I came across Guillermo, the principal of the highly-regarded American Mennonite School. He was ambling down the street with his brother, who was the physical education teacher at the school. I set down my bags of potatoes, onions and bananas and shook Guillermo's hand. "You have a fine son," he said. "We've really enjoyed having him."

"Thank you, but I need to ask you something," I said, trying not to be too confrontational. "Why doesn't he get more homework? My younger son is doing a lot of homework."

Guillermo laughed. "We've decided homework is passé."

"Really?" I tried to laugh back at Guillermo. "That's surprising."

I said goodbye, picked up my groceries and headed to the bus stop, shaking my head. How in the world could the vaunted American Mennonite School decide that homework was passé? I knew there were studies in the United States that supposedly showed that if homework were a drug regulated by the FDA it would be banned as completely ineffective. But I didn't know such thinking had made its way to Colombia.

On Tuesdays and Thursdays I usually took Mario to soccer practice, which was right after school. He and I were both getting more confident about him travelling around La Mesa alone. He had starting taking the bus alone or with a neighborhood friend to tennis lessons, which were later in the afternoon. But the buses did not go all the way up the hill to his school. And I certainly did not want him walking alone on the highway. So on soccer practice days I would pick him up at school in a taxi and we would ride the short distance from the school to the stadium. We would eat a picnic lunch at a little store near the stadium and then go to practice.

One day I sat down in the shade of a tree that grew near the stone bleachers to watch. I was thinking about running some laps around the weedy track at the stadium but the sun was very bright and I had forgotten my sun glasses and my big floppy hat. Two other mothers were having an animated conversation, and I couldn't help overhearing.

"My little brother had it rough as a kid," said one of the women. She was slightly overweight and had dark, bushy eyebrows. Her skin was the color of coffee with a little milk. "He was small for his age and the older kids always stole his lunch money. He was so traumatized by the bullying that he failed first grade and had to repeat it."

"That's terrible!" her friend said, her voice showing her sympathy for this woman's unfortunate kid brother.

The story continued. "Then he did better for a little while but my mother lost her job and couldn't pay for him to finish fifth. He had to go back the next year and repeat fifth grade also."

Repeating a grade or two is actually not very unusual in Colombia. There is no social promotion (moving a child up a grade to keep him or her with his age group) and students failed, or as they said, "lost the year," or "threw out the year," on a regular basis. During our sixteen years of marriage, Saúl never mentioned "losing a year," but when the subject came up at dinner with Gloria one night, she told us how Saúl did really badly in eighth grade. As the year wound down, the teachers were considering failing him. One of Saúl's cousins, Juan, decided that the solution was to change the grades on Saúl's report card. Noticing that Saúl's report card had been tampered with, the teachers were so furious that they decided he would definitely flunk eighth grade.

So while I knew the brother's story was not very unusual, I still was feeling sorry for him as the sister related the boy's travails.

She continued. "But he persevered and went to college and now he teaches social studies at El Liceo Campestre."

As she finished the story I looked around at her face again and realized her bushy eyebrows were exactly like el Profe Francisco's. I smiled to myself. But I did not say anything. By then the sun was a little lower and I decided I could start jogging without burning myself too badly.

Thirteen

TEAMWORK

Since we had the fever for soccer and we believed in ourselves, we decided to challenge a school in Santa Marta to show off our soccer talent and we set the time for 4 p.m. on a sandy field. We never should have opened our mouths. They handed our heads to us, since the heat reduced us to ashes. It was a miracle we did not end up in the hospital for sunstroke and dehydration. We had never suffered such a terrible defeat in all of our high school soccer careers but we deserved it for being too proud and the coastal players gave us a clinic with the ball. They were so fast in that infernal heat. Oscar, who was not a soccer player, consoled us with the compassion of a friend who felt bad about seeing us so sick from discouragement at the defeat, told us: "You know the winners in the loss, my children. Remember, up there in the high plain, the things would be a lot different with the cold and the altitude."

From Saúl's 2004 letter

The disappointment was not unexpected. The twenty-something men who played soccer on the cement soccer field in front of my town house almost every night had been playing soccer since childhood. They were fast, highly skilled, and fiercely competitive. To make matters even worse, they played with what they aptly call a "micro" soccer ball. It's smaller and heavier than a normal ball. So on the rare occasions when they let me join the game, I was not only outclassed on skill, but I felt as though I needed glasses to see the ball and when I kicked it with the force I used on a normal ball, it did not go as far as I meant it go.

I knew I should have just given it up. After all, even the local guys in their 40s don't try to play with these young men. But every night they gathered on the two long cement steps in front of my house and discussed whether they'll have enough players for a game. I kept hoping.

I was a volleyball player in high school and for a few months in college, but soccer became my passion in my mid 30s. Back in Pennsylvania, I played soccer at least two nights a week with my over-30 women's team, Blue Thunder. All through my husband's debilitating illness with cancer, and in the years after his death, running around a field trying to master the elusive goal of playing good soccer has been the best way to distract myself from my struggles and to make me feel as though I can manage life as a widow and a single mother.

Three times a week here in Colombia, Mario and I rode the bus to the soccer stadium by the high school and I did laps while his team practiced. I kept an eye on the practice in case the coach needed a partner for a kid or another person to help with a drill. But he was very self sufficient and I was probably more of an annoyance than anything. So when the preparations for the nightly "micro" game started, I couldn't help but hope for an invitation. One night in January I got my hopes up. It was just after the New Year holiday and the neighborhood college girls were home for vacation. If they decided to play with the men, they would sometimes include me.

"Are you going to play?" I said to them, as the gathering was starting.

"Yes," one of them said. "You can play, too."

I ran upstairs to change. But when I got outside, the men had wandered off, looking as though they had decided not to play.

"What happened to the game?" I asked.

"Well, they decided not to play because you are a woman," one of the 20-something guys said. I was surprised that he was so forthright. I went back inside. I threw a pile of the clothes in the washing machine and washed the dinner dishes. In the meantime, I couldn't help strolling to the window to watch as the guys raced up and down the field, passing, defending and shooting with their usual vigor.

"Mom," Gabriel said. "Don't watch if it's going to make you feel worse."

I was checking my e-mail as the soccer game wound down. "Doña Rebecca, can you play volleyball with us?" I heard through the window. It was Paola, a twenty-something woman who loves volleyball, though the fact that she always plays barefoot or in slippers hinders her mobility. Volleyball doesn't give me the adrenaline rush that I get from soccer, but it was better than nothing so I went to the window and said I would be right out.

"We're going to have three teams and you are a captain," Paola said to me when I emerged from my house as several young men strung up a volleyball net on the erstwhile soccer field.

Because of the holidays, many of the faces on the volleyball court were unfamiliar visitors. I knew my neighbor, Maritza, the mother of a teen-age friend of my sons' and a physical education teacher at the local high school. I called her name and asked her if she knew any of the other players. She mentioned John, who struck me as rather apathetic. I had caught a glimpse of short, pony-tailed Manuel warming up with a good set, so I chose him. I was not too optimistic about our chances. I hadn't played volleyball in months and I was unsure about the other players. But Maritza decided on the lineup, made sure we had a setter, and borrowed a fifth player from another team.

As the third team, we had to play the winners of the first game. I felt a little rusty at first, but John turned out to be on fire. He not only hustled and hit the ball well, but he served with the power and precision of a trained volleyball player. Manuel, who I later learned was a tennis pro, moved well on the court and played great defense. We were winning the game and I started to find my feet. Manuel gave me a beautiful set, not too close to the net. I had time to swing my arms and jump and hit the ball hard. It banged onto the pavement on the other side of the court. "Muy bien!" a teammate yelled. Maritza ran over to slap my hand in congratulations. A few serves later. We won that game. Then we won another.

I started to lose myself in the game. An errant ball was about to drop onto the pavement. I dove, knocked it up into the air, and rolled back onto my feet. I stood up with blood on my knee and gasps of astonishment from my fellow players. I had forgotten we were playing on pavement and that I was not wearing the knee pads I had worn when I came off the bench for the University of Massachusetts junior varsity team in 1980.

At about 11 p.m., everybody, myself included, was tired. Almost all the players wandered off the court.

"Let's play beach," Paola said to me, Maritza, and Fercho, a twenty-something guy who had been playing well all night. I was tired, but I loved the idea of the additional exercise of a two versus two game before calling it a night.

"Okay," I said, and began walking to the other side of the court without thinking about it.

"No, Rebecca. It's you and I against them," Maritza said, pulling me back onto her side of the court.

We're going to end this great evening of volleyball by getting hammered by two youngsters, I thought.

As it turned out, the game was very even. Fercho was fast and by the far the best setter on the court. Paola can pass and hit but she was somewhat of a handicap on his team because she is not much of a runner. Maritza and I were both covering the court as well as we could and trying to set and hit.

We were playing to 15 points and tied at 13 to 13 when it was my turn to serve. I've never mastered the overhand serve, but I have some control and power in my underhand serve. Shamelessly going for the win, I dispatched two hard serves to the corner near Paola. She was unable to return either.

Maritza and I walked to the net to meet the youngsters. "I can't believe you guys beat us," Paola said. Maritza and I looked at each other and laughed. A few minutes later, I was in the shower. As the cold water washed over my shoulders, I smiled. The night had ended much better than it began.

Fourteen

SAÚL'S HANDPRINTS

I remembered the last words of Don Simon Bolivar: "If my death contributes to the end of parties and the consolidation of nations, then I will go peacefully to my tomb." Can you imagine what Bolivar would say if he could see where we are now in Colombia, still at all-out war even now? Just as enslaved as when we were a colony of Spain, but more poor and with even more violence, all at the mercy of capitalism, globalization, and under a military regime that is disguised as a democracy.

From Saúl's 2004 letter

"*M*om, you made a few mistakes here and there," Gabriel said as we walked out of the Mennonite Church of Teusaquillo in Bogotá. I had filled in for one of the delegation hosts as an interpreter for a discussion with a Colombian pastor. The pastor, who had been a pilot in the Colombian air force, had used a few phrases that I did not know as he described his decision to leave the Air Force and dedicate himself to showing Jesus' love to rural Colombians. But I had muddled through and was fairly pleased with my performance.

"Thanks," I said to Gabriel as we turned down the street to walk to the hotel. "Your words of support and encouragement are much appreciated." I thought it was great that Gabriel had followed the pastor's words *and* my translation carefully enough to pick up on my errors. But I kept that to myself.

As co-director for Latin America for the Mennonite Central Committee, Saúl travelled constantly to Colombia, Brazil, Bolivia and Jamaica. Gabriel and Mario remembered the soccer jerseys he brought home from his trips, but they didn't really understand what it meant to promote peace and development.

In most countries, MCC sets up partnerships with local organizations that have the expertise and the contacts to make sure that programs are effective and donated dollars aren't wasted. Saúl would help supervisors in each country make decisions and serve as a liaison between each country's program and the main office in Akron, Pennsylvania. In addition, Saúl helped to place service workers—usually from Canada or the United States—in jobs associated with MCC-supported projects in Latin America.

I didn't expect Gabriel and Mario to absorb all the bureaucratic details of Saúl's work, but I thought they were old enough to understand at least that Saúl worked with good people to try to solve intractable problems of poverty and violence in Colombia and other countries.

Bonnie Klassen, the MCC country representative and an old friend of Saúl's, knew we were living in La Mesa so I don't think she was too surprised when I called her to ask if she had any ideas about MCC programs that the boys and I might visit.

"We have a delegation coming to tour several local projects," she said by telephone. "You should come along—especially to the Fruit of the Andes. Saúl helped them get their latest fruit dryer."

I had expected to follow along with the tour group, but a few days before the tour began, Bonnie sent me an e-mail asking if I could fill in as an interpreter for the meeting with the pastor. At the meeting, Mario and Gabriel listened intently as the pastor recounted how he felt God calling him to leave his well-paid job within the Colombian military to minister to the victim's of Colombia's long civil war.

"I would often speak out of turn to the politicians and generals on my plane, telling them about Jesus," the pastor said. "But little by little I realized that those conversations were not enough, that I needed to leave that comfortable existence and do something more."

The day after the meeting with the pastor, we joined the delegation scheduled to Fruit of the Andes, a fair trade dried fruit company that Colombian Mennonites had founded with the help of the Mennonite Central Committee in the United States. Saúl had helped coordinate the shipment of one of the company's massive fruit drying machines.

Visiting such a tangible example of Saúl's work in peace and development seemed like a wonderful way to help Gabriel and Mario understand what their father did while he was alive. I had never been a big fan of dried fruit, but I love mangos and I was excited about getting a chance to sample the company's products.

The bus pulled up in front of a small nondescript brick building in the south of Bogotá. We crossed the sidewalk and were ushered by a room filled to the rafters with crates of mangos and pineapples. We entered a larger room where several women were furiously slicing fruit and laying the slices out on large sheets. Giovanni Hernandez, the president of the company, handed puff shower-type caps we were required to wear for hygiene purposes.

"Do I really have to put this on?" Gabriel—ever fashion conscious—muttered to me in disgust.

Unfortunately Gabriel would soon have worse problems than having to wear a white shower cap in public. Both Gabriel and Mario inherited their father's sensitivities to smells, and the odor of sweet, ripe fruit was thick inside the small, not so well-ventilated brick building.

Giovanni was showing us the large metal fruit dryers and explaining how they worked.

"It takes about eight hours to dry the fruit," the guide was saying.

"Mom, I feel sick," Gabriel said to me with a look of dismay on his face. "The smell is not good."

"Hang in there, sweetie," I told him. "We're going upstairs soon… But we need to get a picture of us in front of this fruit dryer."

I handed the camera to one of the people in the delegation and got together with the boys in front of the fruit drying machine. Then we went upstairs to Giovanni's office to hear more about the company. We crowded into the upstairs space, where there was an office as well as an area where the dried fruit was packaged and sealed into attractive ziplock bags.

Giovanni explained that each woman earns more than the minimum wage, plus benefits and scholarship money so she can study if she wishes. "The idea is not that she is here chopping fruit for the rest of her life," he said.

I was interested, but I felt a tug on my elbow.

"Mom, can I go outside?" Gabriel asked. "I still don't feel good."

I took both boys back outside to the bus. They agreed to wait there together to see if Gabriel's nausea went away.

When I arrived back upstairs at the meeting, the moment I had been waiting for had come. "Why don't you try these samples?" said an accountant as he walked into the room with a big tray.

First I dried the dried banana. Unlike the crunchy dried banana we are used to in the United States, this was slightly brown but deliciously sweet and moist.

The dried mango slices were tougher but wonderfully flavorful.

The dried papaya was also delicious.

Finally the accountant passed around little balls of chocolate.

"And what do you think of this?" he asked.

I thought it was the most delicious chocolate covered raisin I had ever tasted.

It turned out they were not raisins but were chocolate-covered physalis (also known as gooseberries), a tart-tasting little red fruit that I was unaware even existed.

"I can sell you each a few bags to take home as samples," the accountant said. This was music to my ears. I bought the two bags of mango slices and two bags of mixed fruit. Then I headed back out to the bus to see what the boys were up to.

Unfortunately, Gabriel and Mario were gambling, a pastime I had hoped they would not learn in Colombia. Gambling is very big in Colombia, and it starts early.

School children dig a small hole in the dirt and then take turns throwing the coins toward the hole from a designated spot. The person who manages to land his coin in the hole gets to keep everybody's money. It's a nasty game that can earn a punishment if students are caught playing it at school, but Gabriel and Mario had nonetheless learned the rules and were happily gambling with each other on a little piece of grass next to the sidewalk.

I didn't like the gambling game, but I didn't complain. After all, I was the one who brought them to Colombia, moved into an overcrowded barrio full of children who were pretty much left to their own devices, and enrolled them in schools. Who was I to criticize them for absorbing an aspect of the culture I found distasteful?

"Boys," I said. "Let's get on the bus. I want you to try some of the samples I bought."

We took our seats on the bus and I passed them the bag of dried mangos.

Their reactions were typical.

Mario, who is more adventurous about food, chewed and swallowed his slice with pleasure.

"I like it," he said. "Can I have another?"

Gabriel, who doesn't usually enjoy new tastes as much as his brother, was more noncommittal.

"Yes," he said. "It is pretty good."

Later that day I wasn't sure whether the trip had been worthwhile. But I was confident it was important to continue making the effort to learn about Saúl's job and his commitment to working for peace in Colombia.

Ironically it was our bus driver who inadvertently helped with our education. In fact it was he who really brought the message home.

During our trips back and forth to Bogotá we had noticed that some of the buses had video screens, and once or twice the drivers had decided to show an old movie. Usually the screens were blank.

But on the way back from Fruit of the Andes, the driver showed a new documentary that had just been published by *Semana* magazine, which is like *Time* or *Newsweek* of Colombia.

The bus driver decided to present a documentary on the recent history of terrorist attacks, assassinations and kidnappings in Colombia.

As the sky darkened and the bus headed through a high desert area before beginning the descent toward La Mesa, the video began by describing the dirty war that was conducted against the Patriotic Union, a political party that was founded by the leftist guerillas after the signing of a peace treaty in the 1980s.

Almost every one of the guerillas who came down out of the mountains and to accept the government's offer to work through the political process peacefully was secretly assassinated. Even as the assassination campaign continued a leftist lawyer from Bogotá, Jaime Pardo Leal, agreed to run for president at the head of the Patriotic Union.

Pardo Leal was returning to Bogotá from a wedding near La Mesa when gun men—who were never arrested—shot up his car and killed him.

I gripped the armrests in my seat.

Gabriel and Mario were sitting in front of me in the crowded bus. I hoped they couldn't see the screen.

It got worse—if that was possible.

The screen showed half-naked people trapped behind barbed wire, eerily reminiscent of Hitler's concentration camps.

"The guerilla's campaign of kidnapping moved into high gear," the announcer intoned. "Politicians, business leaders, even ordinary workers found themselves trapped in the jungle with little hope of release."

The bus turned back and forth, down through the dark mountains. By now I was sweating, even though the night was cool.

For the first time since we arrived in August, I seriously considered just packing our bags and leaving in the morning. I was trembling as the bus finally rolled into the stop near Comfenalco.

We grabbed our suitcases and headed down the road toward the neighborhood. As scared as I was, I still had this silly hope that the children had been busy with their video games and had not noticed the terrifying documentary.

I was especially concerned about Mario, who I had tried to shelter from some of the more terrifying aspect of Colombia's history; he was only 10 and prone to nightmares.

"Were you watching the movie?" I asked.

"Yes Mom, I saw the whole thing, and now I'm really scared," Mario said as he trudged down the dark road, dragging his little wheeled suitcase. I felt terrible about not being more forthright with the bus driver. I could have asked him to turn the TV off. I tried to comfort Mario.

"I'm sorry Mario. I feel bad that you saw all that. I've read books about that history, but seeing it all in living color was terrifying," I said.

As usual, Gabriel chimed in with his contrarian viewpoint.

"But Mom, I thought it was so interesting," Gabriel said. "I wanted to stay on the bus all the way to Girardot."

"No!" I said, having to laugh at Gabriel's detached fascination with the documentary. "Two more hours of that would have put me over the edge."

That night, Mario stumbled half asleep into my bedroom at about 9:30 p.m. "Puedo ormer contigo?" he muttered. *Can I sleep with you?*

"Of course, sweetie," I said, opening my mosquito netting and pulling back the blanket. "Go back to sleep. We're safe."

Fifteen

THINGS FALL APART

In a small station, when we were all asleep, we were awakened by military orders. Many soldiers got on to search the train. They started to dig into our things without saying anything and they just pointed their rifles at us if we had questions. When they finished, one of them said, "Everything is okay, my sergeant!" I did not know what he meant and I thought the worst, that we were going to be screwed. Nevertheless, the signal was that many troops could get on the train. Many soldiers started occupying all the free space in the train and later a long line of them in the central corridor. We were all frightened with so many armed people and they were all packed in with us. The soldiers were very young including some who looked even younger than we were. The train started again. Nobody said anything. In Colombia in those times there was mandatory military service which included us. It was a big dilemma that we needed to face when we returned to the high plains. We had to decide if we would do our one year of obligatory military service or pay to get a document saying we had fulfilled the requirement, as long as you were not chosen to serve.

The experience of having so many soldiers traveling with us for almost the whole night, made us remember the interminable war in the country, which for us in that time was not real, it was something about just a few guerrillas that were loose. But we could read the eyes of the soldiers, their fear and their seriousness at being victims of a military structure of death. One more time in my life, I felt impotent and angry about being harassed by a brute force that ran the country without alternatives for a democratic peace and a better future for the people. That night we could not sleep until finally many of the soldiers got off after we passed Barrancabermeja and we could return to breathing the hot, dry air and calm our minds. We slept and when we woke up we thought that it had all been a nightmare but the eyes of the soldiers studying us for so many hours, reminded us that it was not a dream, that was the real Colombia, going back and forth between rifles and sporadic combats, a Colombia with a millennial conflict over a problem of injustice. It was not a nightmare and with sadness we discovered that Colombia was not the stuff of dreams.

From Saúl's 2004 letter

"Who is going to be the coach?" asked Betty, the fearsome president of Comfenalco, our neighborhood. Betty was a short, brown-haired no-nonsense high school math teacher and serious ping pong player whose presidency of the neighborhood had been marked by complaints about her dictatorial leadership style. It was after dinner late one evening in March. About 12 boys, including Gabriel and Mario, were sitting on the stone bleachers in front of our house. They were being unusually quiet and cooperative. Betty had called the meeting to organize teams for the upcoming inter-neighborhood games. The boys had enthusiastically signed up, given their birthdates and their home telephone numbers. Enough boys had signed up to form two teams, one of older boys that would play in the Under-15 division and another of younger boys who would play in the Under-11 division. They chose captains and then came the moment of my anointing. It wasn't as though the boys had much to choose from. I was the only adult around.

"I need to put a coach down for each team," Betty said. All 12 pairs of eyes turned to me. "Señora Rebecca!" they yelled, nodding enthusiastically. They were all clearly pleased that the problem of needing an adult coach for each team was so easy to solve.

I was not quite so thrilled. I had enjoyed teaching soccer to the boys over the Christmas vacation, but I knew some of them were hot-headed and hard to coach. Plus I knew next to nothing about the rules or the norms of Colombian micro-soccer or of the so-called inter-neighborhood games.

"Where were the other parents, especially the dads who are physical education teachers?" I said to Gabriel after Betty dismissed us and we went inside to get ready for bed.

"Mom, you know they're tired of kids after being with them all day," Gabriel said he as squeezed toothpaste onto his toothbrush. "Everybody was happy that you were there."

A few days later I started organizing practices and trying to teach the boys to play together as a team. They were all pretty good soccer players, but they tended to stand and watch the person with the ball, instead of working together. "Carlitos and Mario, you two are the first idiots—I mean the defenders," I said one afternoon while I set up a keep away game (comparable to Monkey in the Middle) in which four players would try to keep two defenders from getting the ball. I had learned how four against two forces everyone to work hard in order to be successful in many United States coaching classes. In Colombia, I had already learned that the monkeys in the game of Monkey in the Middle are known as *bobitos*, or idiots. "Let's not say bobitos," I said. "Let's say defenders."

I told the defenders to carry a plastic cone instead of wearing the nylon vests we used in the United States. The only problem was that when it was time for a defender to switch places and join the four trying to keep possession of the ball, the players flung the cones through the air like Frisbees, delaying the game and annoying the coach. "Just hand over the cone, Carlitos!" I yelled.

I became so engrossed in trying to get the two teams ready for the inter-neighborhood tournament that I almost forgot that our visas were going to expire at the end of April. I finally remembered and called the Colombian State Department.

"I just need to add two months to our visas because of an error they made at the Consulate in Washington," I said.

"Well you need to call back after 2 p.m., when the agents are available to help you," the secretary said.

I called back at about 2:30 p.m.

"I'm sorry; the agents have gone to lunch."

I called back at 4:30 p.m.

"I'm sorry; the agents are gone for the day."

The next day, I remembered to call at about 3 p.m. and explained my situation to Esmeralda.

She said: "We can renew your visas. You need to bring an apostilled copy of your husband's death certificate."

"Okay," I said.

"Also, apostilled copies of your children's birth certificates," she added.

"Got it," I said, taking notes as my heart went into my shoes.

"And of course, apostilled copy of your widows' pension certificate."

I hung up, furious with myself for not insisting that the Consulate in Washington fix *their mistake* a year earlier. Apostilles, which are seals issued by state governments that certify the authenticity of the notary who verified the signatures on a document, took weeks to obtain in the United States. I didn't even know how I was supposed to get them while living in rural Colombia. I had obtained a version of the apostilled widow's pension certificate, but I seemed to have left it in storage in Akon. Why had I believed "Pedro's" lie, "That will be easy to fix in Bogotá?"

I stewed about the situation for a day or so and then called Esmeralda back.

"All the information that you are talking about is on file at the consulate in Washington," I said. "Can't you ask them to send you copies?"

"Sure," Esmeralda answered, making me think for a moment that the problem was not as huge as I thought. "I'll do that and call you back next week."

That weekend our Comfenalco neighborhood teams were to host a team from a rival neighborhood, the Town of the New Century. Julian, the captain of the Under-15 team, had planned games at school. Ironically, the same Julian, our captain and our best player, stopped by our house the night before the game to say that his mother wanted him to travel with her the next day and that he would not be able to play.

"What will we do if we only have five kids?" I asked Gabriel, thinking we needed to have six on the field at a time.

"Relax mom, in Colombian micro soccer, it's four field players and a goalkeeper," Gabriel said.

The Town of the New Century players showed up promptly at about 1:30 p.m. and began warming up. They had nice uniforms, matching socks, and excellent soccer skills.

Germán, a Comfenalco dad with the lean physique and short hair of a serious athlete, had started helping with the coaching. At game time, we gathered all the players together. "Señora Rebecca is going to give you the indications for the game," Germán said, without giving me a warning.

I stood there completely tongue-tied. For a moment, I wondered what an "indication" meant in this context. I realized it was a pointer. But I still stood there silently while the boys looked at me expectantly.

"Uh German, why don't you go over the positions we're going to play?" I said, weakly.

"Okay," he said. "I need two tough guys to stay back on defense."

Gabriel's hand shot up. But my heart went out to him. He was only 12 and most of the New Century Town boys looked older and tougher.

"Okay Gabriel and Juan Camilo, you be the defenders," German said.

By then I had found my tongue.

"You guys will do fine," I said. "Just talk, hustle to the ball, and try to keep your shape. Delay the forwards instead of stabbing at the ball." The pre-game speech finally began flowing.

The game was fast-paced and exciting to watch. The teams were well-matched skill wise, but the Town of the New Century goalkeeper was fearless. He dove onto the hard pavement, stopping or deflecting many of our shots. Our goalkeepers were larger and less athletic. One of our goalkeepers' was nicknamed Clifford because his hangdog eyes and somewhat jowly, albeit handsome face had an uncanny resemblance to the big red dog. Clifford was not afraid of the ball; he was just slow to react sometimes.

After yet another shot got by Clifford's leaden feet, one of the neighborhood moms yelled at me—as if it was my fault. "Rebecca, get Clifford out of there!"

The criticism stung, but I made myself ignore it. After all, where was the yeller when I was trying to train all these players on my own? Germán sometimes helped, but his son was younger, and since a third team of younger boys had been formed, he had his hands full with that age group. At the final whistle, the score was 9 to 9.

"That was pretty good, considering we played without Julian," I told the boys.

But the two fathers quickly deflated whatever feelings of satisfaction I had. "I should take the older kids and have Andres take the younger kids and you coach the babies," German said.

⁓

On Monday afternoon, my phone rang. My heart leaped when I realized Esmeralda was actually calling me back. "I have the file on your visa application," she said.

"That's fantastic," I said, thrilled that something was going right.

"Well, the bad news is that they did everything wrong in Washington," she said. "They never should have given your children visas in the first place. They should be Colombian citizens through their father."

I thought of the 50-year-old Colombian civil war and the forced recruitment into the military of Colombian teen-age boys.

"I think citizenship is a right that they have; something they can claim if they decide to do so as adults," I said to Esmeralda, trying not to sound defensive.

"Well, you really should apply for their citizenship now, rather than trying to get visas for them," she said. "I'd like to see an apostilled copy of your husband's death certificate, and apostilled copies of their birth certificates, and apostilled copies of your marriage certificate."

I cut her off.

"We just want to stay here until June, when school ends. Isn't there another solution?"

Esmeralda thought for a moment.

"What you can do is apply for two 30-day safe conduct passes," she said. "All you need for those are three by four centimeter pictures, your passports, and the fee."

The Safe Conduct Passes were available at the Department of Administrative Security.

"For the second safe conduct pass they just need to call over here and make sure it's okay with us," she said cheerfully.

The safe-conduct passes seemed like a simple, albeit time-consuming solution. But I was still furious with the Colombian Consulate in Washington. I wrote a letter explaining what a complicated situation their error had put me in. I asked for their help. Then I got their fax number off the Internet and faxed the letter to Washington from the Telecom office in La Mesa.

I explained to the children that we had to get permission to miss school in order to go to Bogotá for our documents. "We'll make it a fun outing," I said. "We'll do some shopping and go to the movies in Bogotá. I would also love to go to the international book fair."

I had been reading stories in *El Tiempo* about the authors and events that would be featured at the approaching book fair. A few days later we were sitting on the comfortable chairs at the international section of the Department of Administrative Security on one of downtown Bogotá's wide boulevards. Bolivians, Venezuelans and the occasional Brit roamed in and out. As advised, we had arrived at 7:30 a.m., and after an hour, we had our safe conduct passes and the rest of the day to do as we pleased.

Our favorite mall in Bogotá was an elegant four-story building with a huge atrium. We munched on snacks from the Juan Valdez café on the first floor and then roamed around the stores, mostly window shopping.

We took a taxi to the Convention Center that was hosting the book fair. It was huge, with children's books taking up one entire building. The Colombian equivalent of Barnes and Noble, the Panamerican book store chain, had its own building. We roamed around, picking up a book about the massacre at the Palace of Justice by one of Saúl's favorite authors, Germán Castro Caycedo. We found a copy of a children's book that Gabriel and Mario had loved when they were little. We walked around among the hordes of school children who were being bused to the fair and let loose to explore with minimal supervision.

We were surprised to find a large booth of all English books hosted by an English book store in Bogotá called Authors. We browsed for a while and I chose Khaled Hosseini's novel, *A Thousand Splendid Suns* and Gabriel found a few books for himself.

Our last stop was a floor filled with booths offering technical and scientific books. "This does not look very interesting," Gabriel said.

"We'll just take a quick look around," I told him.

Between shopping at the mall and at the book fair, I was almost out of money, anyway.

We stopped at an environmental organization's booth and I saw something I really wanted for my father, *A Guide to the Bird Sounds of the Colombian Andes.* It was an expensive seven-CD collection compiled by the National Biodiversity Inventory. My father and his wife, Diana, were serious bird watchers who regularly spent entire weeks marching through the wetlands of Costa Rica or Mexico looking at birds. I thought it would be great to support environmental work in Colombia and bring a meaningful souvenir home for my father. But there was a problem. The little set cost 80,000 pesos, or about $40, and I only had about 60,000 left in my wallet.

I remembered seeing an ATM at the entrance to the building. Without a second thought, I hurried down to the entrance and withdrew 200,000 pesos. I bought the bird sound guide and still had plenty of money for that night's movie and the bus ride home the next day.

After we returned to La Mesa, Gloria came over for dinner. We were talking about how well our stay in Colombia had gone. "My mother did not think you would last two months," Gloria said. "'She'll be running home shortly,' she said to me when you first arrived," Gloria said, between spoonfuls of my latest recipe, a rich, beef broth-based soup made with an especially flavorful South American tuber called aracacha.

"Everything has exceeded my expectations," I said.

At bedtime, we pulled out the book we had rediscovered at the book fair, *Willy the Magician,* and relived old times. Gabriel and Mario had both loved the way Willy counted the steps on his way to his bedroom, and always *had* to be in bed before the toilet finished flushing. The book contains beautiful, humorous illustrations of Willy, who appears to be a chimpanzee, dribbling a soccer ball around larger, stronger gorilla soccer players. It even has a ghostly soccer dad who gives Willy magic soccer shoes. I read through the book and was amazed at how happy and yet nostalgic Gabriel and Mario were. I was usually the one who remembered their adventures as toddlers. "Now I'm going to read it to *you*," Gabriel said.

The next morning I headed into town with my shopping list, as usual. My first stop was at the ATM at the Banco de Bogotá. I monitored my bank accounts in the United States by Internet and always made sure there was plenty of money in my checking account, which I was certain currently held about $1,500.

I keyed in my PIN number and waited for that pleasant whirring sound of pesos being mechanically counted. Nothing.

Instead, the machine printed out a receipt that said, "Insufficient funds."

I didn't panic. ATMs in Colombia were sometimes broken. That was probably the problem.

I went across the street to the ATM at the Banco Agricola.

"Insufficient funds."

This time I panicked.

I ran to an Internet café and logged onto my bank account.

The moment my account came up, I saw to my horror that someone had emptied out the account in a series of 11 transactions that had taken place the night before and that morning. The last transaction, the removal of $5.70 had left the account with 90 cents.

I went from being panicked to really scared. What if this person had access to the other accounts? I ran from the Internet café to the Telecom office and quickly sat down in front of one of the old telephones in the back of the office that was assigned for international calls. As other callers loudly poured out their woes to children and relatives in other countries, I dialed my bank's 800 number.

"Enter your password. Followed by the pound sign," The computer voice said.

I looked at the keypad and realized it only had numbers, no letters.

Calling up some kind of super-human power I didn't even realize I had, I entered my password just by remembering where the letters were supposed to be.

As soon as a human answered, I explained the situation and she transferred me to the security department.

"We will freeze that account," said a young woman with a strong Filipina accent. "You need to fill out an identity theft affidavit and mail it to us."

I also put maximum daily withdrawals on my Money Market account, something I should have thought of earlier. By the time I had gotten through to a human and sorted out as much as possible, I had been on the phone for about 30 minutes. I hung up and went to the counter.

"That will be 20,000 pesos (about $10)," said the woman behind the counter.

"I'm sorry, but the reason I was on the phone for so long is because thieves stole all my money," I said. "Can I have until this afternoon to pay you?"

I felt terrible about asking this of the young woman, especially knowing that I had berated her on more than one occasion about the whole "Unlimited Telephone Internet" fiasco.

"Okay, but I'll be in big trouble if I have to close my register short in the evening, so be sure and be here this afternoon," she said with a slight scowl.

As I wandered back toward the bus stop, I was in a state of shock and I was mystified about how the thieves had stolen my money. Betty, the Comfenalco president, appeared on the street, seemingly out of nowhere. I told her how devastated I was by what had happened. "But Becky, it is just money—money you can probably get back," she said, turning me around and pointing me toward the closest bakery. "The important thing is that nothing happened to you or your children. Let's go get some coffee."

I followed Betty's orders, just like everyone else in the neighborhood. We sat down at a red Formica table and a young waitress (one of Betty's former students) brought us coffee. I sat there, sipping my coffee and feeling horrible about the theft but grateful for Betty's company and words of wisdom.

It was hard to know what to do first. After relaxing with Betty for a little while, I went back to the Banco Agricola. A tall executive type with curly black hair and a black moustache was standing outside saying goodbye to a customer. I waited for a moment and then explained what had happened. I mentioned that I had used my ATM card at the book fair in Bogotá. The bank executive did not seem very surprised.

"There was probably some kind of electronic surveillance device on the ATM at the book fair," he said, regarding me with sympathy.

"But the book fair was about a week ago, why would thieves take a week?" I asked.

"It takes a few days to get the counterfeit card manufactured," he answered. "It's called cloning."

"While I try to figure this out can I get a cash advance on my VISA card?" I asked. "Sure," he said. "The amount depends on your credit card."

I got the cash advance and paid back the long-suffering Telecom clerk. Then I went home and logged back onto my bank account. I realized the ATM at the book fair was the property of Colpatria, one of Colombia's largest and most prestigious banks. I called the number on the website and asked to speak to the head of security.

"It seems as though thieves cloned my ATM card last week at the book fair and stole almost three million pesos," I started.

"We'll send some people over there to have a look," Jorge said.

"Aren't you even going to say you are sorry?" I asked, growing frustrated with everyone's ho hum attitude about my loss.

It was a stupid question. I had lived long enough in Colombia to know that people seemed to think that apologizing was a sign of weakness.

"Really, my question is, how do I get a police report that I can send to my bank?" I said.

"Go to the prosecutor's office and fill out a complaint there," he answered.

By then it was too late to go back into town. I tried to forget about the situation for a little while and focus on what I needed to teach my soccer players.

During the game on Saturday, I had noticed that some of them were hesitant to take shots with their left foot. At the beginning of the practice, I began to explain how important it was for them to be able to shoot on the goal with both feet. You can fool defenders and goalkeepers by shooting unexpectedly with your weaker foot, I said.

"I have scored a lot of goals with my *cerdo*," I continued.

They looked at me blankly. "Mom!" Gabriel said laughing. "Left foot is surdo, with a U. You said cerdo which means pig!"

Gloria came over after practice and I told her about the theft and the banker's suspicions. "I've tried not to frighten you about all the different dangers in Colombia," she said. "Otherwise I would have warned you about not using ATMs in Bogotá."

The day after I discovered the theft I went to the prosecutor's office and she handed me a thick form titled "The Unique Form for Criminal Information."

"I'll help you fill out this part," she said, entering the date and the legal description of the crime. She flipped over the first page and gestured to the blank narrative section of the report. "Here you need to think of yourself as Gabriel García Márquez, or what was his name? Ohhscar Wilde?" she said, drawing the O in Oscar out longwise. "Put in as much detail as possible."

I was on my way home to write my great crime story: *The Chronicle of a Theft Foretold*, when my cell phone rang. It was Gabriel.

"Mom, can you come and get me? I don't feel well."

I hurried over to the American Mennonite School and found my way into the first aid area, inside the teacher's room. Gabriel was sitting on a narrow examining table with five students crowded around him and a glum expression on his face.

His forehead was a little warm. I took him home and sent him to bed. I wasn't too worried. Gabriel had always been a little susceptible to fevers. But the next morning he was miserable, very hot and weak and with pain in his legs.

Ever since I had first come to Colombia with Saúl I had been hearing stories about dengue fever, a mosquito-borne illness that is prevalent throughout South America. But I always thought Colombians exaggerated the threat and attributed every little fever or headache to dengue.

I had avoided reading too much about the illness; I felt as though Colombians talked about it too much. "My dear friend is in the hospital with dengue; he's bleeding profusely from his anus," my new plumber had told me months earlier—three minutes into our first conversation.

Just a few weeks earlier, *El Tiempo,* the daily newspaper whose articles about the latest kidnappings, massacres and battles I read compulsively every day, had as usual, thrown in some advice for its readers. A long article had counseled the thousands of capital dwellers to be extra vigilant about travelling to La Mesa and other points south during the Holy Week vacation. "Don't let dengue ruin your trip to the warmer climates," the article had said.

Seeing Gabriel lying in his bed, occasionally rubbing a hand over his aching knees and moaning, made me think I finally had to admit that the dengue threat was real. I got on the Internet and went to the World Health Organization's website. "Dengue is a mosquito-borne infection that causes a severe flu-like illness, and sometimes a potentially lethal complication called dengue hemorrhagic fever." That was something I had heard, but it was scary to see it in black and white. The website went on to say that the threat of dengue is growing every day. The mosquitoes which spread dengue thrive "where household water storage is common and where solid waste disposal services are inadequate."

I thought of the way my neighbors feared water shortages so much that they tended to build huge water storage tanks. I had seen Doña Mercedes' tank; two or three children could have had a nice swim in it. I doubted it was properly covered to prevent mosquitoes from using it as a breeding ground.

I called the clinic above the supermarket and asked what to do if I feared my son had dengue.

"Take him to the hospital to have his platelets checked," the receptionist said, as though she got the question all the time.

The dreaded La Mesa hospital. Since our first week in La Mesa, people had warned me to avoid the hospital. "My wife was there, very pregnant and sick," a missionary friend named Aaron told me early in our visit. "I left to bring her food and toilet paper. When I tried to get back in I was told visiting hours were over. It was terrible. I knew my wife was suffering."

So with trepidation I bundled Gabriel into a taxi and we went to the hospital. It was housed in an old white building on the south side of town. Dr. Ricardo attended us quickly and seemed very nice and very knowledgeable. An efficient phlebotomist had no trouble drawing Gabriel's blood. The ease with which she found Gabriel's vein reminded me of all the times Saúl had his blood drawn. Sometimes it went smoothly and sometimes nurses poked and prodded for a while before they finally drew blood from Saúl's once well-muscled arms. After Dr. Ricardo examined Gabriel, the doctor had him sit on a gurney in the hallway to wait for the results of the blood test. There were several children and young women sitting or laying on gurneys in the hallway; most were receiving fluids intravenously. A huge section of paint was peeling off the ceiling, but the floor was clean. I watched as orderlies pushed a peasant farmer on a gurney, with what looked like a huge machete cut in his thigh, down the hallway. Nurses were putting on double masks before entering a room where a patient was coughing and coughing. I thought of tuberculosis.

Finally, Dr. Ricardo came to tell us the blood test showed Gabriel's platelet count was normal, but that he was still concerned that Gabriel had the early stages of dengue.

"I think he does have dengue, based on his symptoms," he said.

"So does he need to stay and get an IV?" I asked.

"No," the doctor said. "Take him home; give him plenty of soup and other fluids. Control the fever with acetaminophen. Bring him back if blood starts flowing from his gums."

The thought of blood flowing from his gums was more than I could handle. I tried to focus on the easy part: take him home and give him soup.

I had to call Ruth, a friend from the neighborhood who was staying at my house with Mario until we got back from the hospital. But cell phone use was prohibited within the hospital. I told Gabriel to wait for a moment and I wandered out into a narrow courtyard. Through windows on the right I could see cooks preparing dinner for the patients. I caught one of the cook's eyes and smiled at her. She came over to the door with something in her hand. "How about some juice?" she said holding out a glass of sweet raspberry smoothie. I gratefully drank the glass and handed it back to her. I called Ruth to give her the news, and then headed back to take Gabriel home.

"Mom, you know that room that says 'isolation' on the door?" Gabriel said, as he carefully lowered himself off the gurney. "The nurses left the door open for ten minutes."

"Oh dear, Sweetie," I said. "Let's try to go home as quickly as possible."

By then the fever seemed to be even higher and his leg pain was worse. I guided him to a bench in the waiting room. There was a tough-looking carpenter there, complaining about how long doctors were taking to remove a splinter from his finger. I almost told him to buy himself some tweezers.

Standing out like a sore thumb amid all the ordinary La Mesa people was a woman wearing a Brooks Brothers-type shirt, designer jeans and carrying a leather purse. "You are not from here, are you?" she said.

I guess she was not the only one who stood out like a sore thumb.

"No," I said. "But we're living here for a year. We came to the hospital because I was afraid my son had dengue."

She looked at him with concern.

"You have to get him out of here—these country hospitals are just not hygienic," she said. "The hospitals in Bogotá are much better."

I thanked her and told her we were on our way.

But there was a problem. Our insurance had not yet agreed to pay for the visit and we could not leave until the bill was paid.

I sat with Gabriel on the hard white bench while we waited for word from the cashier's office. "Mom," Gabriel said. "My legs are killing me. Can we borrow a wheel chair?"

I put my arm around his shoulders. "I think the wheelchairs are saved for people who are even sicker, Sweetie."

I checked with the cashier's office again, but still no word from our health insurance.

Gabriel continued to suffer. Finally I had an idea.

I called Edgar, our favorite taxi driver, and asked him to pull up to the side door of the hospital. As soon as Edgar arrived, I hustled Gabriel out the door with two thousand pesos to pay Edgar for the ride home. "You can't leave without your exit permit!" the receptionist yelled at me.

"I'm not leaving!" I yelled back, turning around and smiling.

I went back into the courtyard to call Ruth again and let her know that Gabriel was coming home alone. I smiled at the friendly cook who had given me raspberry juice earlier. Then I sat down to wait. I looked around the shabby little waiting area, noticing a Frosty the Snowman head sitting on a shelf, apparently left over from the previous Christmas.

My cell phone rang. I hurried back to the courtyard, answering it as I walked.

"Gabriel is okay, but I gave him acetaminophen when he arrived and he vomited," Ruth said. "Don't worry. I'll stay here until you get back."

Finally the cashier gave me my exit permit, meaning our insurance company had either paid the hospital or agreed to pay in the future. I gave the precious paper to the receptionist and walked out into the dark street. A waiting taxi took me home quickly.

My first priority the next morning was making a good, iron-rich beef soup for Gabriel. I hurried to the supermarket, bought a soup bone, and some other soup ingredients, charged everything to my VISA card, and rushed home. Gabriel had slept well but he was still aching and feverish. His gums appeared to be normal, and he said he really preferred Gatorade to beef soup, but I started boiling the soup bone anyway.

Mario finished watching a television show and got right to the point.

"Mom, remember we were going to Bogotá for my birthday hot shower," he said. "Is Gabriel going to be able to go?"

Mario was turning 11 on May 8 and had told me that all he wanted for his birthday was to take a long hot shower at a hotel in Bogotá. I had been amused by the request and assured him I would make it happen.

"He's not doing well, Mario. I'm trying to focus on getting him better."

"But, mom, you promised me a hot shower for my birthday!" Mario said, adopting a rare slight whine to his voice.

"Yes, and we need to go anyway to get the affidavit notarized and mailed," I said. "We just have to wait and see."

Little by little, Gabriel gradually got better during the day. His fever subsided and his leg pain decreased.

"I could make it to Bogotá in a car," Gabriel said the next morning.

I was anxious about getting the paperwork to my bank so I decided to look for a driver who would be willing to take us all the way to Bogotá. The going rate for a trip like that was about $70, but there were special permits for long distance trips involved and most local taxi drivers would rather not take the trip. Ramiro, whose son played on Mario's Under-11 soccer team, said he had a friend who would do it.

The taxi driver dropped us off at the embassy, and we worked our way though the multiple levels of security guards that protect the embassy. After a brief wait, a kind official notarized our police report. "I'm going to look around for a family that is going back to the United States now," Gabriel said, with a wry smile, joking about how he was ready to go home *now*.

It *had* been a tough week. "Let's go to the movies," I said once we were in a taxi after express mailing the affidavit to Virginia. "I might need to charge the tickets since I'm running a little low on cash," I said, opening my wallet to survey the contents.

My VISA card, the only credit card I had brought to Colombia, was not there.

For a moment I could not imagine what I had done with it. I hoped that I had just taken it out at home and left it there. But then I remembered my hasty trip to the supermarket for soup ingredients.

"Let me just call the supermarket, they probably found it," I said, trying not to think about the implications of a lost credit card on top of my cloned ATM card.

"Hola William!" I said when my friend the supermarket manager came on the phone. "Did you by any chance find my credit card in the store?"

"No Señora Rebecca," William answered. "We have not seen it."

My heart sank. But I thought of the saying, "bad things happen in threes." We had the theft, the suspected dengue, and the now the lost credit card. Nothing else bad could happen.

Luckily I had enough money from my credit card cash advance to get us a hotel room for the night with hot running water and bus tickets home to La Mesa. And Gabriel, who had been so frighteningly ill just a few days earlier, was back to normal. I never did find out if what he had was actually dengue or just a bad case of the flu.

In church on Sunday I was thinking about the warm circle of friends at Pilgrim's Mennonite Church in Pennsylvania. We never failed to pass the microphone around the room and let people share the joys and sorrows of the week. At the Mennonite Church in La Mesa, the microphone was never passed around. Pastor Jaime, who was balding and always dressed very properly in slacks, an undershirt, dress shirt and tie, monopolized the microphone completely. Mostly this was annoying, although I loved it when the drummer would strike up a lively rhythm and the pastor would clutch the microphone to his face and start jumping up and down in a credible imitation of Mick Jagger.

But this week a Bogotá theologian was visiting and he had not brought the usual save-your-soul-through-prayer type of preaching. He started by recapping the story from Genesis of Cain and Abel. "Cain took Abel out into a field, killed him and left him there for dead," he said, speaking in smooth, measured tones.

"Here in Colombia the Cain and Abel story happens over and over. How could it be that Cain takes Abel to a field and leaves him for dead and we as a people of faith say nothing?" he asked, the urgency in his voice growing. "Sometimes we have campaigns to win souls. Why don't we have campaigns to win justice?"

I remembered that even without my credit card or my ATM card I was fortunate.

The service ended and Gabriel and Mario came sauntering in from Sunday school. "You missed a fantastic sermon," I said, as we walked across the street to the bakery where we always had snacks after church. "How was Sunday School?"

"It was fine," Gabriel said. "We just played soccer the whole time."

Sixteen

NATURE

Life in general was complicated and full of challenges for us. In our teen-age years, my sisters and I lived in barrio called San Cristobal in our native city of Facatativá, Cundinamarca. It was a time in which burning the midnight oil after spending the day in school was the norm every night, times in which we had to convince ourselves, without hesitation, that we had the power to someday escape the misery and the hunger and manage to be productive members of Colombian society, which was every day more messed up and at war—ever since the invasion of Columbus. I should say that our condition of raw, destitute, plebian struggle in an urban environment going through sacrifices was not as hard as the lives our parents. They burned their lives in the countryside, confronting from dawn to dusk a little rocky patch of land that we dared to call a farm, trying to make it produce a little bit of food or something to sell in the market. Without a doubt, this time of having to study in the city in very limited conditions was one of the most difficult times of my life. Today this is the daily reality for a little more than half of the Colombian population.
From Saúl's 2004 letter

A strange noise woke me up. It was not the usual sound of the bus honking as it goes by our house. Or birds singing on the electric wires near my windows. It was a loud scratching noise. I scrambled out of my bed and ran down in the direction of the noise to the area outside Mario's room. The ceiling there was covered with large white soundproofing tiles. The scratching noise stopped.

I had suspected we had an unwanted, furry little guest in our house, but now that it was clear the guest was bent on destroying the ceiling tile, I realized I had to do something. After breakfast, I called Reynaldo, Gloria's handyman friend who could fix anything but preferred to save souls.

"Hello Rebecca," he said, greeting me with a hug. "God bless you."

I explained about the rat noises and Reynaldo quickly improvised a step ladder out of some pieces of cement, removed one of the tiles and stuck his head into the space between the ceiling tile and the roof.

"I can see the rat," he said, climbing down. "She's pregnant and she's digging herself a nest."

"Really?" I was surprised the animal was still hanging around. I climbed up and poked my head into the space. The rat was sprawled on top of a metal rafter, its little head, one front foot, and its beady eyes poking out in front and its long tail hanging down in back. She looked very unhappy at being caught in the act of a home invasion.

"Can we get a have-a-heart trap and release her back into the wild?" I asked.

Reynaldo looked at me quizzically, waiting for an explanation of a have-a-heart trap. "It's a little box we use to trap pests without hurting them," I said. "I hate to think of poisoning a soon-to-be mother."

"You don't want her to have her babies here," Reynaldo said, carrying the brick he had used as a step ladder back to my laundry room. "I'll get some good poison so she'll get sick, and leave and die somewhere else." It sounded awful, but an entire brood of baby rats in the house were not a pleasant thought, either.

I had lunch with Mario and Daniel, who went to school and soccer with Mario, at a bakery outside the soccer stadium. I decided not to go into detail about the pregnant rat, but the conversation was strange anyway.

As often happens with 11-year-old boys, Mario and Daniel were talking about an unfortunate classmate's intestinal troubles. The owner of the bakery, a cheerful, chubby woman with flowing blond hair, joined in.

"He was probably just uncurdled," she said, coming out from behind her counter.

"Uncurdled?" I asked. "What does that mean?"

"If a child falls hard or jumps off something they can get uncurdled," she said, shaking her head at my ignorance. "Being uncurdled leads to diarrhea. But doctors today, they don't know anything about being uncurdled."

Thinking about how I and the modern medical establishment had managed all these years without knowing about the dangers of uncurdling, we headed over to the stadium. By then I had been watching the two coaches train 50 or 60 kids at a time for months, and it occurred to me that I could offer to help. I walked into the office and equipment room behind the snack bar and found Raúl, the head of the soccer school, sitting at his desk.

"REBECCA THATCHER!" he yelled in his best attempt to say my name with a correct English accent.

Raúl was tall and always sported a bushy moustache and a slight sunburn. His dedication to the soccer players of La Mesa was as unquestionable as his organization was erratic.

"Since I'm always here watching Mario I thought you might want me to pitch in," I said.

Raúl smiled and stood up.

"Yes, I'd like you to train the girls. Teach them some moves with the ball and work on their juggling," he said. "And make sure they know this move," he said, throwing a ball in the air and then catching it between his feet in a way that I found incomprehensible.

"I don't understand what you just did but I understand what you said," I answered as we walked over to pre-practice player meeting.

La Señora Rebecca Thatcher will be working with us now," Raúl announced at the meeting. "She knows too much about soccer."

The girls were less hyperactive than the neighborhood boys, and most of them were experienced players. As I began working with the girls, I noticed that they often seemed to practice in slow motion. Angelica was a beautiful 16-year-old with long curly brown hair and a wide smile. She did not like to run. I was trying to teach them to move to open space when they did not have the ball, and to work as a team to maintain possession, but it was an uphill battle. Diana, who was a little chubby but had excellent skills, was by far the best player on the team. The rest were accustomed to standing and watching while Diana did all the work.

At one point Diana had the ball, but two defenders were closing in on her and she needed a player to get into position for a pass. Sending the ball to Angelica was the best option, but Angelica was ambling so slowly into a position that she was no help to her teammate.

"Angelica, could you at least walk quickly?" I yelled in frustration.

After practice Mario and I stopped by the store to buy food for his school's Adventure Camping outing. The new physical education teacher, Oscar, had worked as a camping guide before coming to the school, so he was planning a weekend-long excursion into a national forest on some mountains east of La Mesa known as the Quinini Ridge. The kids were supposed to pack a tent, a sleeping bag, clothes and all the food and water they needed for the weekend into their backpacks. (Oscar would later become famous in Colombia when he was one of the last survivors in a popular Colombian reality TV show.)

The campsite was about a two-hour hike up into the mountains, the teacher had said. We didn't have a real hiking backpack, so Mario borrowed Gabriel's big soccer backpack, which at least had lots of space and padded straps. Once we had him all packed, all I had to do was figure out how to get him to the town square at 4:45 a.m., when the buses were supposed to leave. The local buses didn't start running until after 6, and most taxi drivers didn't start until even later.

One of Gloria's least favorite families in the Comfenalco was a family I'll call the Godoys. According to Gloria, the mother worked her fingers to the bone as a free-lance house cleaner while her two adult children sat on the couch. Gloria especially could not stand the oldest son, who she frequently accused of selling marijuana in the neighborhood.

"He has ruined the neighborhood with his bad habits," she said many times at dinner. "It's terrible the way that family goes hungry, but it's their fault because they don't work."

The only person in the family to escape Gloria's ire was the second son, who was studying environmental engineering at the university in Girardot. "I feel bad for him, because I know he does not have enough money to eat while he's at school," Gloria said. "I hate to think of him going hungry all week."

Despite Gloria's misgivings, I got along well with all the Godoy kids. I knew the eldest smoked cigarettes, and I occasionally gave him grief for smoking at the soccer court, which was against the rules of the neighborhood. But I saw little evidence that he or anybody else was peddling marijuana in Comfenalco.

I spotted the two younger siblings, Paola and Freddy, outside while I was trying to think of how to get Mario to town at 4:45 a.m. I asked them if they had any ideas.

"We'll walk him there," Paola said with a smile. "Let's see, if he needs to be there at 4:45, we should leave at four."

My jaw dropped. I realized that the only people for whom I had ever woken up at 4 a.m. were my children or my husband.

The next morning Mario and I got up at 3:30 to have breakfast. I realized that if Paola and Freddy didn't show up I'd have to take Mario out of the neighborhood, down the road to the highway, and up the long stretch of highway to the town square by myself. I wasn't so worried about muggers; it was the falling down drunks stumbling home from a night of partying that scared me. But Freddy and Paola showed up promptly at 4 a.m. The stars were shining as we walked up the hill, talking about the plans for Mario's campout.

"I don't understand how they can plan a campout without a campfire," I said, thinking I was glad I had not signed up to be a chaperone.

"It's probably for the safety of the kids as much as it is to protect the nature preserve," Freddy said.

We were among the first to arrive at the town square, but the other parents arrived soon after; some were driving late model SUVs. I reminded Mario to take pictures and kissed him good bye.

When Paola, Freddy and I arrived back at Comfenalco, the sun was just starting to rise. I told Paola to come back to my house in half an hour for waffles. I poured myself a cup of coffee and then got busy whipping the egg whites by hand. By then I could get soft peaks in egg whites in less than two minutes. I set the table with a little bowl of powdered sugar and some pancake syrup from the supermarket.

When Freddy and Paola arrived with their niece, a nine-year-old girl who had been entrusted to her grandmother years earlier, I showed them to their seats and served Freddy the first waffle. "What's this?" he said, stirring the powdered sugar I had passed to him to sprinkle on his waffle.

"That's powdered sugar," I said. "The best way to eat waffles is with a little powdered sugar and a little lemon juice."

All three were thrilled with the waffles and I felt as though I had somewhat made up for them losing a morning's sleep to get Mario to his camping trip.

As I was saying good bye to the Godoys, Doña Mercedes came out of her house, a worried expression on her face.

"A rat just ran through my house and out the door," she said.

"Really?" I answered. "That's terrible."

One of the many pieces of advice Gloria had given us when we first arrived in La Mesa was not to eat in any of the restaurants other than the Hotel Bogotá. She was afraid other local restaurants just weren't sanitary enough for our American digestive systems.

Despite Gloria's warnings and because we had lived in Colombia for months, Gabriel and I decided to go out to lunch. A computer engineer I met at an Internet café said his mother's restaurant, *El Arcoiris, (The Rainbow)* was very good. So Gabriel and I decided to try it. The restaurant was a few blocks up the main road from the town plaza. It had a small courtyard that was filled with an unusual palm tree and other exotic-looking plants. We were both excited when we saw a "Mexican Tray" on the menu.

The waitress soon brought out authentic corn tortillas, delicious strips of beef, pork and chicken, refried beans, spicy hot sauce, pico de gallo, and shredded cheese. Because Saúl and I had met on the Texas-Mexico border, and both our children were born in Austin, we had been fans of Mexican food for years.

"This is wonderful," Gabriel said as he loaded his tortilla with a little bit of everything. "I can't believe we found a place like this right here."

"I must have walked or ridden by it dozens of times," I said.

"I can't wait to tell Mario about it when he gets home," Gabriel said.

When the 60,000-peso bill came I realized I would have to think twice before coming back, especially considering my financial troubles. I had made the advance on my VISA card last as long as possible. And I had exchanged the emergency $200 I had in a U.S. cash for Colombia pesos, but I was running out of options.

Late Sunday evening I headed back into town to wait for the buses to come back from the camping trip. I was hoping Mario had enjoyed himself and managed to survive on the breakfast bars and canned sausages he had packed.

Finally the two buses drove up and Victor Hugo's rotund frame emerged from the driver's seat. "Everything was great, Doña Rebecca," Victor Hugo said with a smile.

Mario climbed down from the bus, looking happy but disheveled with his sleeping bag unrolled. "Mom, I ran out of food and I had no money, but Victor Hugo bought me an *arepa* on the way home," Mario said.

"How was the camping?" I asked.

"We hiked and hiked and hiked," Mario said. "We only slept about 20 minutes at night."

Although I had tried not to worry about Mario spending the weekend off on an isolated mountain ridge. It was a relief to have him home in one piece.

The next week I tried to come up with a way to replace my ATM card or my credit card. But none of the options would work. I hated to do it, but I called my father and asked him to wire me three million pesos (about $1,500) to tide me over until I sorted everything out.

A few minutes later my father sent me two e-mails with the secret code I needed to pick up the money at Western Union. I grabbed my passport and hurried off to the Colmena bank that doubled as the Western Union office.

"Don't you have an identification card?" asked the clerk when I handed her my passport.

"Yes but a passport is all I need, according to Western Union," I told her, reluctantly handing over my ID card, which had expired in April along with my visa.

"Your identification card is expired," she said, looking very pleased with herself. "Our rules state that we can't give you the money."

I had had it with bureaucracies, but I tried to stay calm and I asked to speak to the manager. He emerged from his glass-walled corner office with a smile, and then escorted me in.

"Western Union says very clearly that a government-issued photo identification, such as a passport, is all that is necessary," I said to the manager, a portly man with a glass-windowed corner office in the little bank.

He surprised me by getting as angry with me as I was with the bank. He said that his bank, as an agent of Western Union, had the right to follow its own policies regarding identification requirements. I said that was absurd.

"This is all your fault!" he yelled. "You let yourself become illegal!"

Then he calmed down. "Don't you have a friend with a current identification card?" he asked. "Have the wire transfer sent to her."

I had not yet given Gloria all the details about my financial situation. But when I told her about how I had lost my credit card and asked her if I could have the wire transfer sent to her she remained perfectly calm. We went to the bank the next morning, where the bank insisted that Gloria fill out a form describing her income, assets and accounts. Gloria consented, filled out the form and after about an hour, a clerk reluctantly handed over the money.

I started thinking about how I could manage until the end of June with no credit card or ATM card. I still owed rent, tuition, and other miscellaneous bills. I realized I had bought many items, like my double bed, our television and the washing machine that I could sell. Trying to figure out how much money I needed and what I could sell my possessions for just gave me a headache. It was much easier when money flowed easily from the ATM machines in town.

But all around me families lived this way all the time, trying to decide how to feed and dress their kids on tiny teacher's salaries. I stopped by Don Jorge's store as he was going through long cardboard strips where he kept a neat tally of what each family in the neighborhood owed for food.

"What can I get for you?" Don Jorge said as he put the strips of cardboard away in the cash register.

"With all my problems I might need to get credit pretty soon, too," I said.

"You've still got plenty of money," Don Jorge said. "How are the boys' soccer teams doing? Are they getting better?"

Don Jorge reminded me that we were planning to take all three teams to play at the Town of the New Century on Saturday.

The boys *were* getting better, especially Carlos, our neighbor, had become a much more focused and organized player.

On Saturday some of the parents said it would be cheaper for the three teams to take three taxes rather than two buses to the Town of the New Century because we would have to take two buses to get there, and bus fare had just gone up from 800 to 1,000 pesos—or 50 cents a person.

That made sense, so I called the taxi stand in town and requested three taxis. The kids were wildly excited and they all jammed into the taxis. Andres, one of the dads who had been helping me coach the kids, wasn't ready, so I asked our driver to wait for him. He was just a few minutes late, but by the time we arrived at the Town of the New Century, the other two drivers were waiting at the side of the rundown soccer court looking very upset.

One of them made a scratching motion on his cheek as, if to say that we were all thieves. I was embarrassed and apologized and paid all three taxi drivers. Then I asked the boys why they hadn't chipped in and paid.

"We didn't think we had enough," said Camilo, one of the goalkeepers on the Under-15 team.

"Well you should have talked to the drivers and told them I was coming," I said, knowing that my delinquency would soon be hot gossip at the taxi stand. To further dampen my mood, it began to drizzle as we started warming up for the first game.

Julian, the captain of the Under-15 team, had managed to find some time in his schedule to actually come and play. Again, the Town of the New Century team looked good, with matching yellow socks, blue shorts and white jerseys. But Julian's skill and speed made all the difference. The Comfenalco Under-15 team won eight to two. The Under-11s, despite all my hard work, lost zero to two. The Under-8s won five to zero.

After three hours of soccer and two victories, all of the kids were excited. One of the fathers had arrived with his pickup truck and offered to take the kids home in the back. About 15 kids packed into the back of the truck, chanting "We won! We won!"

When they arrived at Comfenalco, they took a victory lap around the neighborhood. The father was honking his horn and the kids were chanting as loud as they could from the back of the pickup truck.

I rode back more sedately in one of the other father's cars. When I found Mario at the house, I asked him what he thought of the day. "The victory lap in the pickup truck was the best!" he said, smiling.

A few days later, I was back at the stadium trying to help with the soccer practice. Dark clouds were gathering on the horizon as all the players gathered behind the western goal and worked on juggling, or trying to keep the ball in the air with their feet. I am not a very good juggler, but I grabbed a ball and tried my best, counting out loud to show my progress—or lack thereof. "UNO! DOS, TRES," I yelled as I managed three kicks before the ball went flying out of control onto the track that bordered the field. I ran and picked it up and tried again. I ignored the fact that, unlike me, the kids never picked up the balls with their hands to start juggling. They always put their foot on the top of the ball, pulled it back toward them until they had their foot under it, and then flicked it up in the air. That seemed like a skill that would take me forever to master. But as I kept juggling, I could tell I was getting better. "UNO!" I yelled as I touched the ball perfectly into the air in front of me. "DOS!" I said as I did the same with my left foot. "TRES!" I yelled again as I managed to get my right foot on the ball and send it into the air again. "CUATRO!" I said as I went past the record of my previous attempt.

I was so entranced with my own progress I did not notice that the girls I was supposed to be coaching were gathered by one of the goal posts, chatting and just pretending to practice their juggling. I was about to say something when I heard Raúl's booming voice, "Everybody count like Señora Rebecca!" I noticed the girls started trying a little harder so I went back to my own practice, determined to break into the double digits.

As the skies continued to grow darker, Raúl divided the 30 or 40 kids who had been juggling together into different age groups and sent them off to various areas of the stadium to continue practicing. He left me and the five girls in a small area behind the stadium's western goal. I grabbed some cones and placed them in a large diamond shape. I had demonstrated how I wanted the girls to keep the ball moving quickly around the diamond. Instead of stopping the ball to control it, as they were prone to do, I told them to just touch the ball with the insides of their feet so it would continue around the cones. Rain began falling as I watched most of the girls kick the ball and jog on to the next cone. Angelica, of course, continued to prefer a leisurely stroll on the soccer field.

It started raining harder, and I noticed some of the small kids walking through the stadium gates and up to the shelter of the awning in front of the snack bar.

"Can we play now?" Laura asked.

"I'm not sure what to do about this rain," I answered, as I wiped a few warm little drops from my forehead. After almost a year in Colombia I knew that most Colombian mothers did not like their children to get wet or cold in the rain. Once or twice I had tried to explain that colds are caused by viruses, not by rain, but I knew most Colombian mothers were convinced their children could get sick from being out in the rain.

"It's just a little rain, let's start the game," Laura insisted.

"Okay," I said. "We can play a little. I'll be on a team with Angelica and we'll play three against three."

Of course I had forgotten my cleats. We began running up and down the little field, passing the ball as best as we could as the rain poured down harder and harder. My sneakers slipped on the wet grass and I went down, flat on my back. The girls came over, laughing, to pull me up again.

The next time I got the ball, I managed to get away from Laura and I looked up to see Angelica actually walking quickly toward the goal. She was yelling at me for the pass. Despite my slippery sneakers I managed to send the ball to her feet. The goalkeeper, Isabel, came running out to grab the ball a second too late. Angelica had already tapped it past her with a perfect kick. Isabela then collided with Angelica and both girls crashed down into the mud.

155

They stood up again, laughing. Angelica raised her muddy arms in triumph and shouted, "GOOOOOOL!"

Meanwhile, all the boys' teams that had been practicing walked past us and hurried to the shelter of the snack bar. We kept kicking and running and laughing. Finally, I looked at my watch and realized it was time to go. We gathered up the cones and the balls and walked up to the snack bar. We were exhausted and exhilarated.

Seventeen

COFFEE

Not much time passes without thinking of a particular family crisis when the resources ran out and we arrived at two critical weeks where we just didn't have anything to eat. Simply, the money ran out, the provisions ran out and we were too embarrassed to go around asking for food. Hunger hounded us to the point that we could not sleep well. I remember that in the yard of the house somebody had planted cabbage and it had grown pretty well. I think it was the manna of salvation; I said if the cows live on grass then why not try to pacify our hunger with this old cabbage since nobody seems to be planning on eating it? We cooked that cabbage in water and flavored it with salt and a little bit of oil, later we ran out of oil and we ate it just with salt. Later we ran out of salt and it was just plain boiled.

If I remember correctly, cooked cabbage was all that I ate for seven straight days. Ever since, all through my life, Brussels sprouts and cabbage have been a symbol of the importance of not forgetting what it is to be hungry. When I can I go to the supermarket and buy some cabbage and cook it the same way, boil it, put on a little oil and salt and eat it like that. It's like my only spiritual ceremony to remember not only my own experience but also to be able to prayerfully taste and think of the millions of people in the world who go hungry and even die of hunger in many countries.

From Saúl's 2004 letter

*W*e were standing inside the bus terminal in Ibagué, a provincial capital about three hours by bus from La Mesa, and had just received news that made our hearts sink. We were hoping to catch the next bus across the Line, the nickname for the highway across the Central range of the Andes from Ibagué to Armenia, the heart of Colombia's coffee-growing region.

"The Line is closed—at least for today," a ticket seller said.

It was less than a week before we were scheduled to fly back to the United States, and for the moment we were stuck halfway between La Mesa and soon to be 13-year-old Gabriel's birthday wish.

About two weeks earlier, as our year in La Mesa drew to a close, we were eating our usual Thursday night dinner at Gloria's: rice and vegetables, well-done beef, and plantains that were sliced and fried so they looked like French fries and a salad of cucumbers, tomatoes and avocado. Preciosa, Gloria's Dalmatian, was barking softly from the patio where she was confined at meal times. Gloria had cooked the same supper for us when we first arrived. "This is the *best* dinner," Gabriel said. "The rice is fantastic."

Gloria made the exact same menu for us every week for the entire year.

"What would you like for your birthday?" Gloria said as she cleaned her plate with an alacrity that reminded me of Saúl. My husband and his siblings all ate very quickly—a legacy, I imagine, of the scarcity they endured as children.

Gabriel thought as he pushed his avocado and tomato salad around the plate with his fork.

"Let's go to the Eje Cafetero!" he said to my surprise.

To this day I don't know where Gabriel came up with the idea. But it was a great one. The Eje Cafetero, or Coffee Axis, which might be more understandably translated as the Coffee Growing Region, is famous for its quaint villages, verdant hillsides, and most of all, the national coffee park. As the crow flies, the Eje Cafetero is only about 80 miles west of La Mesa, but the Central range of the Andes can prove to be a serious impediment. For one thing, the range includes the fearsome Ruiz volcano, which stands 17,457 feet above sea level and which erupted in 1985, killing the entire town of Armero—21,000 people.

"If that's what you want for your thirteenth birthday, we'll just have to do it," Gloria said decisively that night.

Over the next few days I checked out budget hotels on the Internet and sold the guitar that Gabriel had lost interest in playing. My ATM card was still frozen and my credit card had never been recovered, so money was still a little tight. We economized in ways that had never occurred to us—like walking back and forth to town instead of taking the bus. We also sold our color TV and our washing machine as our departure date approached. We had to make the $1,500 last.

Instead of sensibly staying home and calmly getting ready to say our final *adios* to Colombia, we were heading off for an adventure. It seemed vaguely appropriate.

Saúl never wanted to say *adiós*. He outlived his terminal diagnosis for months, and refused to admit that he was going to die. "Dear God," he wrote in April, when his right hand was becoming almost as badly paralyzed as his left hand. "I just want to think about life; it's as if my whole being refuses to waste any time thinking about or imagining my death."

Saúl's refusal to contemplate his death meant that we lived those last few weeks fully, inviting friends for feasts, going to soccer games and listening to good music. Then Saúl began alternating between unconsciousness and delirium.

"We need to help the sailors who can't afford to travel home," he said as he lay in a recliner in our living room, his organs slowly shutting down and his level of consciousness gradually receding. "We should start a communal fund." Even when he was delirious, some of the things he said sort of made sense.

I called Saúl's parents at their farm in Colombia. This was before thieves stole their telephone lines for the copper and they still had a land line. "If he becomes conscious, or even semi-conscious, I'll call you," I said.

After a few days of lapsing between delirium, unconscious and moments of lucidity, Saúl began straining to breathe during the night. We had an oxygen machine ready but he refused to allow the little tubes from the oxygen machine anywhere near his face. The hospice nurse suggested we add anti-anxiety medication to the high doses of narcotics I was already giving him for the pain in his back and legs. She told me the anti-anxiety medication sometimes helped patients deal with the "air hunger."

I sat beside Saúl's bed as he gulped for air and moaned in pain. "Do you want a pill for breathing?" I asked, knowing that Saúl's moral standards—even in this state of weakness and illness—might prompt him to decline a pill if I said it was for anxiety. "Yes, a breathing pill," he gasped. He swallowed the Ativan and drifted off. I fell asleep on the couch next to him.

In the morning the house filled up with people. My father and my step-mother, Diana, arrived from Texas. Saúl's oldest friend from Colombia, Timothy Stucky, flew in from Arizona. Eligia, Saúl's sister from Washington, had been staying with us all week. Two of Saúl's cousins, who were nurses in New York, came to help care for him. Saúl's administrative assistant at the Mennonite Central Committee, Kathy Martin, had been keeping Saúl's friends and family informed all throughout his illness.

"Becky?" Saúl said, suddenly opening his eyes.

I dialed the farm as quickly as I could. "Sweetie, your dad wants to talk to you," I said. I pressed the speaker button and set the phone down on my husband's chest.

"My dear son, I'm sorry you are so ill." My father-in-law's pain-racked voice boomed into the room.

"No. I'm fine," Saúl answered weakly. "Don't worry about me."

No sooner had Saúl said those words than he fell back into unconscious-ness. My father picked up Gabriel and Mario at school. They came into the living room and regarded Saúl with a little fear and a little acceptance.

I gave them each a hug and said, "Pappy spoke to his father this morning." They nodded and went upstairs to play on the computer. That afternoon, as I sat on the bed next to Saúl's recliner, wishing for one more moment of lucidity, Saúl took one last breath and then closed his mouth, seeming to go in peace.

I sat there and cried for a few minutes. I suddenly understood why women hover over their loved ones bodies for hours, bathing them and arranging them in shrouds. But after crying for a little while, I wiped my eyes and went upstairs.

"Sweeties," I said, and the boys stopped playing their computer games and looked up expectantly. "Pappy died."

Both boys threw themselves onto the nearest bed and wept with abandon. I walked back and forth between them patting them on the back and trying to comfort them, knowing that there really was no comfort in a moment like that.

Somehow, we got through the rest of the afternoon. I found myself in a funeral home that evening, choosing a plain wooden coffin and answering questions about Saúl's birthplace, age and profession. The next morning I a wrestling match Gabriel and Mario were having with my brother Mark. I told them to sit down and rest for a moment. "I am going back to the funeral home with clothes for Saúl," I said, showing them the Colombian national soccer team jersey interrupted I had found in his closet. "Is there anything you want to put in the coffin with him?"

"We definitely need to send a soccer ball," Gabriel said, tracing the soccer ball on the front of the jersey. "You've got the jersey. Now he just needs a ball and some soccer cleats." Gabriel rushed off to rummage around in the garage.

Mario did not say anything. He took down his favorite art project, a paint-by-number creation of a puppy and a soccer ball and a framed picture of himself. I wanted to question the puppy painting—Mario had worked on that for hours and it was a labor of love, but I wasn't sure it was precisely what Saúl needed by his side. But I remembered that I had a picture of the painting and I agreed to let Mario put it inside the coffin. We took the items to the funeral home and came home to get ready for the burial, which, in keeping with Colombian custom, was held the next day.

At the memorial service, which was held four days after Saúl's death, Saúl's love for coffee was a running theme. About 200 people filled the main sanctuary at a large Akron church to remember Saúl in stories, hymns and prayer. Daryl Yoder-Bontrager, who, with Saúl, was co-director of the Mennonite Central Committee's Latin America program, remembered asking Saúl at his job interview what was the worst thing that a co-worker could do to him. Saúl had just flown in from Austin to interview for the job of being Daryl's co-director, and he maintained his sense of humor. "The worst thing anyone could do to me is bring me a cup of decaf coffee," Saúl deadpanned.

Saúl got the job as Daryl's co-director and over the next few years he and Daryl developed what Daryl said was the best working relationship that he had ever had with a colleague. The two started off travelling through Colombia and Venezuela, working intensely as they surveyed projects and evaluated personnel. After their trips, they'd meet in the office, pour their coffee, and try to find solutions to the problems they had encountered. "After our cups were full we'd talk, and keep on talking until after the coffee was long gone. Those talks were where we really did the stuff of our work, praising some in MCC Latin America or Caribbean, talking through how to handle difficult personnel problems, deciding where to cut budgets or where to increase budgets, figuring out how to maneuver through the sometimes murky waters of Latin American Mennonite politics," Daryl said.

Daryl, who came to our house often as Saúl gradually succumbed to cancer, remembered that on the day Saúl died he looked at Saúl's empty coffee mug on his desk and wanted to throw it across the room. "But mostly I just looked at it, feeling as empty and dry as it was. Coffee drunk by oneself is barely worth drinking."

Kent Dutchersmith worked under Saúl at a Mennonite Voluntary Service program in Indiana in the 1990s. When Saúl came to Kent's house in Indiana, Kent was horrified to discover that he only had decaffeinated coffee on hand. He made a pot and served Saúl a cup, hoping Saúl would not notice the difference.

Saúl took a sip, looked squarely at Kent, and said, "I forgive you."

Considering Saúl's love for coffee, it made sense to try to get to the Eje Cafetero before we left. But what makes sense and what is possible are sometimes two different things. The trip to Ibaqué, the last city before the highway that crosses the central range of the Andes, went smoothly. But heavy rains the day before had caused mudslides on the highway to the Eje Cafetero and officials had closed it.

"Maybe tomorrow," a ticket seller told us.

We checked into a hotel and spent the next day wondering around Ibagué, which is the capital of the state of Tolima and known throughout Colombia for its musical heritage. We ordered the famous Paisa Plate at one of Ibagué's traditional restaurants. I think the Paisa Plate was originally designed for the nutrition needs of field workers or perhaps mountain climbers. It's a huge amount of food—beans, rice, sausage, a fried egg, a fried plantain, steak, a corn tortilla and sometimes five or six other dishes. Mario and I shared one but couldn't quite finish it. Gabriel, of course, loved it. "This is fantastic," he said as he gobbled down most of his Paisa Plate.

The next morning we were hoping that The Line would be open. But the clerk at the hotel was pessimistic. "I just heard on the radio that it's still closed," he said. "You should stay another day."

"Thank you," Gloria said. "But we'll check out and go to the bus station to see."

After we were out of earshot of the clerk, Gloria told me she thought the clerk was lying. "He just wanted our business for another night," she said as our taxi drove through downtown Ibagué to the bus station. But when we first arrived at the bus station, it seemed as though the clerk was right. One bus company told us The Line was closed. As did another. But then a third bus company said The Line was open.

"Now I don't know who to believe," Gloria said.

We wanted to go, but our flight home to the United States was a week later, and we did not want to get stuck on the other side of the Andes. There was a lovely outdoor coffee bar outside the bus station. It had a simple half-circle cement bar around a small kitchen where baristas furiously brewed coffee or espresso. They also had blenders for smoothies and milkshakes. We decided to sit on the stools and order drinks while we thought about what to do. Surely a nice cup of coffee would clarify everything. As we were ordering, Gloria spotted a police officer and hurried over to talk to him. She came back to the coffee bar looking more confident.

"He said The Line was open, but that at times it's only open in one direction so there are delays," Gloria explained. "I'm not sure if we should go or not."

Mario put down the iced coffee smoothie he had been enjoying and said he was game. "Let's go!"

We bought tickets on the next bus scheduled to leave, an old green contraption with four open seats in the back. I gulped down an anti-nausea pill. I now knew that sometimes my stomach could not handle high speed, switchback turns.

Our ears popped as the bus climbed back and forth up toward the high crossing. We sped by workers who were repairing mud slides and farms that doubtless contributed to the instability of the soil. "What are they thinking planting bananas on such inclines?" Gloria said as we passed a spot where an entire hillside planted with bananas had slipped down onto the highway. Twice the bus had to stop because one lane was closed, but each time we waited only about twenty minutes.

We crossed a high spot where the steep sides of the mountains were shrouded in mist and then started heading down. Suddenly a huge swath of the Eje Cafetero was laid out before us in a beautiful green valley, with just a few cities and towns scattered here and there.

We found a small, clean hotel on the outskirts of downtown Armenia. The next morning we arrived outside the park before it opened. That gave us time to visit a horribly tacky tourist store outside the park. Gabriel, who by then had completely mastered some of the cruder aspects of Colombian slang, and was inclined to repeat with great pride expressions he learned in the streets such as, "That didn't last any longer than a fart in your hand," delighted in taking pictures of all the crude wall hangings and signs at the story. "Look mom!" he said, "This is so funny. It's a sign to hang in the bathroom: Think when you take a crap. That way when you need to think, you won't crap it all up." There was another one he liked, carved into a cross-sectioned slice of a tree trunk: "I'll trade you a motorcycle turned into shit for a wheelchair."

Finally the park opened and we were able to tear ourselves away from such a marvelous example of Colombian culture. We climbed up into the observatory tower so we could see the park, which stretched out into the distance with coffee fields, amusement park rides, chairlifts, exhibits and restaurants. We took a long walk on a trail that took us by different types of coffee plants and explanations of how they are grown. We carefully inspected a spooky indigenous burial ground. We wound up at a model Colombian coffee farmhouse, where a sweet gentleman showed us around and started to explain how coffee is grown, harvested, dried, shelled and roasted.

Gloria interrupted him. "Been there. Done that," she said.

We continued on to what attracted Gabriel and Mario: the rides. Gloria and I ordered coffee while Mario and Gabriel road on a roller coaster, and drove the bumper boats and the go carts. Gabriel was determined to win the go cart race. He drove around with his foot all the way down on the accelerator and steered with grim determination. He could not catch the leader, however, until the final lap, when he squeaked by him just before the finish line.

After a huge lunch at the food court and more sight-seeing, we headed back to our room in Armenia.

"I'd love to go on to Pereira," Gabriel said that night as we were talking about our day over huge dishes of ice cream.

"When you come back next year, we'll take a longer trip, continue on up to Manizales and Medellin," Gloria said.

"That will be great!" Gabriel said. Although Medellin was once a notorious drug-trafficking capital, it is now known for its efficient subway, tidy streets and cultural landmarks.

The next day we were riding a large bus on the last leg of the trip back to La Mesa. Suddenly we heard a thumping sound and the bus pulled over.

"We have a flat tire," the driver said. "But we should be able to get it fixed in ten minutes."

The four of us wandered across the street to a snack bar and bought sodas and chips. None of us thought for a moment that the tire would be repaired in ten minutes, so we relaxed on chairs outside the snack bar, marveling about how well our trip had gone.

I noticed a large furry animal tied to a telephone pole across the street and I couldn't help but laugh. Saúl loved *chiguiros* or capybaras, the largest member of the rodent class in the world. They are funny looking, fairly gentle animals that live in the wild in Colombia and other Latin American countries. They are considered good to eat and were officially decreed to be fish by a Roman Catholic bishop in colonial times so they could be eaten on Fridays. Colombians still eat capybaras.

"Mis chiguiros!" Saúl would say when he arrived home from a trip and was excited to see his children. He used to read a charming Colombian book to them about a *chiguiro* who wanders around confused about why all his friends are laughing at him. Finally the *chiguiro* realized that he had a huge piece of straw sticking out of the top of his head.

"I *have* to go take a picture," Mario said, surprising me because he is usually so unsentimental. I handed over the camera and walked across the street with Mario.

"Do you remember how Saúl loved *chiguiros*?" I asked.

"Of course," Mario answered. "He used to call me a chiguiro."

After Mario had taken several photos we strolled back to the snack bar and sat down. The bus driver's assistant had started a wrestling match with the bus driver. Clearly, the two of them also had no hopes of the tire being fixed rapidly.

But eventually the tire was repaired and the bus driver called us over to board and we finished our trip to La Mesa. Now all I had to do was pack everything back into my six suitcases, make sure Crystal's paperwork was in order, and get on a plane.

Of course leaving was not simple. Our kind veterinarian, who had been so good to Crystal all through our visit, promised he would complete all the paperwork needed for her to get onto the plane and go back to the United States. But at the last minute he admitted that he hadn't done the paperwork. "You have to take her to the airport to have her examined there," he said. "All I can do is give her the rabies shot."

It was nerve wracking to have to worry about Crystal and her paperwork in addition to frantically giving away almost everything we had accumulated during our year in La Mesa, saying goodbye to as many people as we could, and finally, loading the six suitcases back into Edilberto's truck. We left early in the morning on June 29, 2008, because we had to have Crystal checked at the veterinary's office at the airport. Crystal passed her physical exam easily and soon was once again sitting anxiously inside her crate at the airport. We sent her on her way along with the six suitcases and then ordered a delicious breakfast at the airport restaurant.

My dear brother Mark met our plane at the JFK airport and drove us through the night to our house in Akron, Pennsylvania. It felt good to be home. I couldn't wait to visit Saúl's grave. I had so much to tell him.

Epilogue

It has been five years since our family returned from our year-long Colombian adventure. I went there wanting my children to spend time with Saúl's family, learn about his native country, and improve their Spanish. When we returned from Colombia, we gathered all the boys' report cards from their Colombian schools and went to reregister them at Ephrata. We were a little disappointed that nobody even glanced at the form showing that Mario received Es for *excelente* in English and Physical Education and Gabriel also received Es for "personal cleanliness" and "posture." Despite our eagerness to show off the boys' Colombian grades, the officials just took the boys' names and enrolled Mario in sixth grade at Ephrata Middle School and Gabriel in the eighth grade. It seemed as though the ease of the paperwork foreshadowed the ease of the transition back into Pennsylvania life. The boys did well in school, rejoined their soccer teams and appeared to be happy and healthy. We kept in touch with friends from Colombia through Facebook and eagerly looked forward to returning every other year.

I have continued to save the cold water that comes out of the tap in my shower in a bucket, and then use it to flush the toilet. Water in the United States is cheap and plentiful, but I see this daily routine as my little meditation on the preciousness of water—and life—that I learned during our year in Colombia.

A year or so after returning home I discovered that people with a college level knowledge of English and Spanish were needed to work as court interpreters. I failed the first written Spanish test. Among other transgressions, I mistakenly said a tool is masculine, when tools are feminine. I studied by reading and taking courses and retook the written test, which involved rendering a written Spanish translation of an English legal document. After that I had to take four more tests, each of increasing difficulty, until by June of 2012 I became a fully-certified judicial interpreter in the Commonwealth of Pennsylvania. Ironically it was me who profited from the hours of Spanish practice during our time in Colombia. Of course the young men also benefit because I can provide nice little extras like clothes, food, utilities and college tuition.

Meanwhile, Gabriel and Mario have transformed from the cute boys I took to Colombia to powerful young men who are making their own ways in the world.

Saúl's life, and the way we honored him by spending a year in his country is something we talk about frequently. We fondly recall the food, the adventures, and the friendships. When we return every two years we reconnect with relatives and friends with whom we built strong relationships during the year. The impact of the crazy idea that Flor gave me in the summer of 2005—"Why not bring them here for a year?" back when we were still in the throes of grief—is immeasurable.

Acknowledgements

This book was mostly written under the supervision of Jami Bernard, a brilliant writer, editor, and teacher in New York City. For about three years, I took Jami's online writing courses and she tirelessly tried to turn me into a writer who conveys emotion in her work. Any emotion that the reader detects here is to her credit. I was a newspaper reporter all my life, and habits die hard. My classmates during those years, Cara Coslow, Janis Garza, Melissa Spiers, Griffin Shea, Amy Nathan (the author of *The Glass Wives*), Christina Gombar, Anita Bryant, Kathryn Kemp-Griffin, and Griffin Shea, to name just a few, were fantastic and yet encouraging critics. I hope to read all of their books soon. Many people made this trip possible, most importantly, my sister-in-law, Gloria, who was unfailingly positive throughout what must have been—at times—quite an ordeal. It meant so much to me that my mother, Susan Thatcher, came to visit us half way through the year. My father, James Thatcher, very generously sponsored the last month of our stay after my money was stolen and I lost access to the bank. Both my parents were amazing during Saúl's sickness. My brother drove us back and forth to the airport and took wonderful care of our car during our absence. We might still be trying to load up suitcases if it weren't for the packing skills of my dear sister-in-law, Eligia Murcia. Rich Landis did a wonderful job handling my correspondence during the year I was away. My wonderful stepmother, Diana Seidel, was an early supporter of this book and sent several pages of corrections. Connie Leas, the author of *The Art of Thank-You: Crafting Notes of Gratitude, Fat: It's Not*

What You Think, and *Your Hands: How They Shape and Reveal Your Nature*, gave the manuscript a thorough vetting and had many helpful suggestions. I want to thank my dear friend Peggy Fogarty-Harnish, whose entreaties of "I want to read this book" have inspired me to finally put it out there. And finally, this is my memory of what happened—augmented by a journal—I apologize for any errors that may be included.

Readers are invited to go to www.facebook.com/SeekingSaul to get updates about the book and join the mailing list.

26071654R00103

Made in the USA
Charleston, SC
22 January 2014